ight First & Every Time

Managing quality in projects
and programmes

Right First & Every Time

Managing quality in projects and programmes

John Bartlett

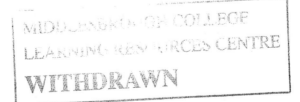

Project Manager Today
P U B L I C A T I O N S

Project Manager Today Publications
Larchdrift Projects Ltd, Unit 12, Moor Place Farm, Plough Lane, Bramshill, Hook, Hampshire RG27 0RF

First published in Great Britain 2005

ISBN 1 900391 13 9

British Library Cataloguing in Publication Data
Bartlett, John, FAPM
 Right First & Every Time: managing quality in projects and programmes
 1. Total quality management   2. Project management
 I. Title
 658.4'01
 ISBN–10: 1900391139

Printed and bound in Great Britain by Antony Rowe Limited

Acknowledgements

My thanks go to Ian Seifert and Ken Lane for proof-reading the manuscript and providing valuable comments.

Foreword

In this book John Bartlett has crafted a first-rate addition to his previous books on risk management and programme management. This is a suite of 'must haves' on any project and programme manager's bookshelf.

Well written and logically developed, the book cuts to the core of defining and managing 'day-to-day' quality throughout the whole project and programme cycles. Planning, implementing and controlling quality throughout a project and, indeed, beyond formal project delivery is clearly linked to the tenets of sound governance.

A particular strength of this book is the useful methodology of defining quality through the use of innovative tools such as 'quality definition mapping' and 'quality definition workshops'. The book rightly exhorts managers to recognise that setting stakeholder expectations is essential to maintaining the quality impetus but, importantly, it offers insightful ways for capturing, setting and communicating stakeholder expectations.

For me, the setting down and development of the nine quality maxims by harnessing specific quality drivers demonstrate the practical value of this book.

Overall, this is a no-nonsense and very readable practitioner's guide amply underpinned by a robust theoretical framework. It will serve the needs of project and programme managers extremely well both now and for a long time to come.

John Daly
Principal Lecturer, University of Portsmouth, Business School

Preface

There are many books on quality. So, what makes this one different? The difference is that it focuses solely on quality from a project management perspective. It does not, for example, attempt to deal with the subject of quality process control in steady-state business or the continuous improvement of business processes. Rather, it focuses on those transient projects and programmes that change business, construct or refurbish something – IT projects, business change projects, construction projects, research and development projects, for example.

This book does not, therefore, discuss the history of the Quality Movement, the principles of SPC, TQM or Six Sigma. These subjects more appropriately belong to the areas of continuous quality improvement and are quite adequately covered in other publications on quality.

I believe, though, that project and programme managers need a publication that will help them to understand how to manage and achieve the often neglected member of the triple project constraint – quality (the others being time and cost). That is the purpose of this book.

It is interesting to note that many project management methodologies mention the need to manage quality in projects, but very few give any practical advice on how it can be accomplished. Many also advocate the need to construct a Quality Plan, for example, but again, few show how this can be constructed. How many projects these days even have a Quality Plan? More importantly, how many project managers have experience of producing one? In this book I demonstrate how a good, standard

Quality Plan can be produced and how it can be used as a prime, controlling document for achieving project quality.

The very human activities of requirements agreement and expectations setting are a key focus of this book. Interestingly, for many projects, these activities are often not envisaged as being linked to quality. However, I demonstrate that these are fundamental activities for achieving the desired levels of quality in any type of project.

This book will, hopefully, address the shortfall of good, practical advice in managing quality specifically for projects. It reflects my own experience of striving for quality in projects and programmes in over 30 years of business.

John Bartlett

Navigation

This book has been written in a roughly chronological sequence of activities, where quality is defined, planned, controlled, tested and implemented. It is recognised, though, that readers will want to be able to reach specific activities quickly, so navigational guidance is given here.

Use the **Contents** to see the sequence of main subject headings.

Use the **Glossary** to find the chapter most relevant to a particular subject.

Use the **Index** to find the page of a specific item.

Use the table at the end of the **Introduction** to review the nine 'quality maxims'.

Contents

1

Introduction

The old adage 'If a job's worth doing it's worth doing well' admirably demonstrates the difference between having quality and not having quality. 'How well does the job need to be done?' is a question that might be asked at the start of any project, since the amount of quality required is a direct consequence of the answer.

Quality is a perception, however. It can mean one thing to one person and something else to another. For this reason it is often difficult to reach a natural consensus on the meaning of quality, so it is hardly surprising that in projects where quality is not given specific attention the final deliverables may be less than expected.

So, what exactly is quality? In everyday life, we do not always need to have an exact definition of quality. It can, for many purposes, remain vague. It is a word used liberally. People speak of 'quality time' in terms of time away from work. I received a travel brochure recently advertising 'quality breaks'; but what does it really mean? There were no qualifying adjectives: the brochure did not say 'good quality breaks' or even 'poor quality breaks', though we assume it implies the former.

As a word, quality is indefinite, yet it is often used in everyday language as a qualifier to denote something higher in status, luxury, excellence or perfection. Manufacturers frequently extol a 'quality product', persons of high standing in society have often been referred to as being 'persons of quality' and workmanship may be spoken of as being of high or low quality.

In terms of luxury, we often talk of a 'quality car', meaning a car that has a higher specification than the basic model and the finish is more luxurious. The basic model, however, can also be a quality car if it meets the requirements of the person desiring it, ie, it is fit for purpose.

For projects and programmes, however, quality needs to be defined. Put simply, if it cannot be defined, it cannot be managed. This is why the definition of quality is such an important early task for projects and why Chapter 2 (Quality definition) gives it particular focus.

In business terms, quality is generally defined to mean 'fitness for purpose'. For projects, this basically means 'meeting requirements'. If someone comments 'This is a quality piece of work' then that person usually means that the work has been done well. This comment on excellence may also relate to expectations. 'I was expecting you to fit only the radiator, but I see that you have also made good the surrounding plaster' is a comment demonstrating how expectations may be exceeded. Is this latter 'fit for purpose', however? Yes, if the requirement is not compromised by the additional work; no, if the additional work took longer or cost more and the customer had not budgeted for this.

This demonstrates that client requirements should never be taken for granted. Even the most obvious expectations need to be clarified. The Millennium footbridge across the River Thames in London had to be closed for several months not long after its grand opening because pedestrians crossing the bridge caused it to wobble alarmingly. For a busy river-crossing in a capital city, a requirement not to wobble would seem obvious. However, when embarking on projects and programmes it is often best to state the tolerances required for even the obvious. Assume nothing and there can be no arguments later.

There are few hard and fast rules for managing quality in projects. All the methodologies state it should be managed, but good, practical guidance is often lacking. Experience shows that it is certainly worth managing, however, since besides quality being a visual result of the end-product it is also an enabler. It contributes to how a project is managed, how resources are marshalled, how time is scheduled, how costs are controlled and how expectations are set and achieved. This is why projects should not ignore it, and not just because it may be seemingly difficult to grasp as a concept or manage as a practical undertaking.

Quality is not confined to a particular project stage. Like risk management it is all-pervasive. It appears in every work package and every action. It is not a function that makes one stop and say: 'Today I am going to tackle quality'. Rather it causes one to think 'Am I tackling this piece of work in the right way? Does it meet or exceed expectations?' Quality should, therefore, be part of a project team's mindset.

There are, of course, discrete stages of a project where quality is more obviously exposed, such as product testing. Here it is possible to switch on particular quality procedures to check that deliverables are attaining the desired level of quality. Apart from these instances, however, quality, in terms of process, must be the retention of a *mental checklist*, continually applied to every action, by every member of the project team.

Risks of not having quality

Why do so many projects not manage quality? One reason, I believe, is that many find it difficult to sell the benefit of managing quality, and to justify managing it in terms of effort and cost. This is probably truer of softer business projects, where fixing the quality of deliverables is less tangible than, say, the construction of a bridge.

Often the best justification is to list the risks of not having quality. History is full of projects that failed through poor quality. However, the risks to a project of not having quality are usually not immediate in effect: a fact which is regularly used as an excuse for not needing to promote quality in the first place.

The long term effects of not having quality, however, are particularly far reaching. This can frequently result in an often open-ended increase in time and cost. For example, the initial cost-saving of, say £15,000, on not producing a user manual to a set level of quality, can result in a much larger ongoing cost over an indefinite period, in terms of wasted effort, negative productivity, disenchanted users and increased calls to the support desk. A direct cost of having disenchanted users is a delay in the provision of benefits.

Cost and time, therefore, appear strongly in any compilation of the long-term effects of not having quality, and consistently manifest themselves as:

- increasing the time in which benefits can accrue
  users take longer to learn the product, longer to become productive in using it and, therefore, longer to become innovative and creative through its use
- increased costs through 'fire-fighting'
  a reaction to unplanned workload through the sudden and costly need to provide additional resources, in terms of fixing problems, providing additional training, documentation and support
- increased time and costs through inefficiency
  poorly planned processes, which cause delays, errors, etc.

Therefore, a risk of not having quality frequently relates to the end-users. There are many developed products that become redundant in the eyes of users almost as soon as they are installed. The failure is not necessarily through the technology of the product itself but through a lack of understanding of the rapidly changing requirements of the users. Fashion is a key consideration of lifespan among product consumers.

The users' perception of what will be delivered is a good indicator of how well any marketing exercise has been carried out throughout the life of the project. The end-product should at least match expectations in terms of meeting users' requirements. It should be usable and work as they expect it to work. If they've been told nothing, their expectations will be set by rumour and the 'grapevine', often to negative effect.

A project that embraces quality focuses strongly on the users themselves: their needs, their expectations, their acceptance and productive use of the product and fashionable tastes. Such a project also considers the full range of stakeholders, many of whom will not be users, but may be sponsors, sellers, marketers, manufacturers, investors, etc. A properly scoped and executed communication plan is, therefore, a vital component for ensuring the right level of expectations of quality.

Justifying quality for projects

A key difficulty that often arises for project teams is maintaining quality under pressure. Even though a project business case may have set out good reasons for attaining a certain level of quality, there will be occasions when a project team will be under pressure to curtail aspects of quality in order to meet specific deadlines. This is fine if the curtailing is done formally through change control, but not if unapproved operational short-cuts are made. The continual maintenance of quality is, therefore, important during a project's lifespan. This is why the role of quality manager, or similar, is an essential role for any project where quality will play a significant part.

The link from quality to change control should always be strong. I often find that projects without good change control also exhibit poor quality. Poor change control usually results in scope creep, which is a major cause of project delay and cost overrun. Therefore, good change control is itself a quality function. The risks of not having it are legion.

The link between quality and risk management is equally strong. In fact, a good risk register will include risks associated with the hindrance to achievement of quality. This, in itself, is good material for any justification for the cost of managing quality in a project, particularly if the risks are quantified. The cost of re-work, for example, is rarely calculated in risk terms, but is a surprisingly common impact in projects, particularly, IT undertakings. Getting it right every time really does have a positive effect on the bottom line. Yet, how many calculate the cost savings of re-work prevention?

In a recent low-value software development project, I was pleased to have a programmer on the team whose duty of care meant a high attention to quality. He raised regular changes during the design of code stage, but they were always positive changes. Typically, he would think carefully about the development of a block of code and suggest building a specialist development toolkit, in order to save valuable development time.

It is rather like a carpenter needing to make a specialist tool in order for a particular job. The emphasis would be on time saved, not only currently but also for the future. Without the specialist toolkit, future changes would take longer to make. The question that always needs to be asked, though, is how beneficial is this additional preparatory work?

This shows that quality not only has to be justified ahead of any programme or project, but also during its execution. Managers will be faced regularly with the need to make balanced decisions regarding time, cost and quality throughout the life of their projects.

I do not like to dwell on the past, but there are clearly lessons to be learned from project failures. The UK's Millennium Dome is a very public example of failings in quality. Construction of the building took place before decisions had been finalised about its contents. A problem, not only because the benefits case relied on the quality of exhibits producing the desired number of paying visitors, but also because the construction couldn't possibly allow for exhibits of a non-standard layout.

In projects, requirements tend to come before the design and build phases, for obvious reasons. Any deviation from that approach risks damage to the end result. It should not be a surprise, therefore, that quality has a direct effect on benefits realisation. However, I am still surprised that many project teams fail to make this fundamental link, and they fully believe that quality can be agreed much later in the project lifespan.

In cost terms, justifying quality is much to do with the appetite of stakeholders for investing in the benefits. The level of quality desired from the deliverables needs to be balanced against the cost of achieving it. For projects, quality comes at a cost, in spite of many who think it costs nothing. It certainly costs nothing to adopt a quality attitude, and mentally to build in considerations for quality into every activity. However, there is a cost in conforming to deliverable requirements and with the associated management overhead to ensure conformance. Table 1 summarises some considerations for the cost of project quality.

In order to understand the true cost of managing quality in a project, it is important to begin writing the project Quality Plan as early as possible in the project lifespan. I advocate opening a Quality Plan in the early stages of discussion between supplier and client. The Quality Plan is then able to form part of the contract and each party will know from the outset the extent of quality

Quality cost consideration	Cost factor
Desired level of quality for deliverables	Deliverable production costs: method of construction, finishing, packaging, transfer
Level of testing for deliverables	Volume and duration of testing; testing approach
Desired level of support for installed deliverables	Training and documentation costs; online versus call centre approaches
Project management	Approaches over and above the methodology for ensuring quality during the project life cycle: people, skills, time
Quality control	Measurement activities desired
Quality assurance	Level of reviews and audits desired
Attitude to quality	Free (unless specific training in adopting a quality mindset is thought to be needed)

Table 1: Some considerations for ascertaining the costs of quality in a project

desired and how it will be measured and signed off. I use the term 'contract' loosely, since it does not have to be a legal contract, but could be a document of understanding between parties. (Refer to Chapter 5 for building a Quality Plan.)

At the programme level, justifying quality is somewhat easier. The economy of scale enables an 'across the board' saving to be made through the adoption of a generic quality approach. Quality assurance, for example, becomes easier, since the programme can fund review teams centrally. QA resources can be procured from outside of the programme through a single point of contact, or dedicated resources can be provided by the programme itself, relieving projects of the overhead of managing QA activities.

Demonstrating the quality concept

It is important that everyone associated with a project or programme has a clear view of the meaning of quality for a particular undertaking. Because, as I have already stated, quality is a perception; everyone will have differing views of quality. These views need to be brought into line and regularly monitored. The method for accomplishing this is via the project communication plan. (Refer to Chapter 3 'Setting expectations'.) However, this assumes that everyone is already sold on the need for defining and managing quality in the first place!

Demonstrating the concept of quality should not be necessary if an organisation already subscribes to an overall quality approach or standard. Otherwise, it falls to a project manager to ensure that all stakeholders understand the quality concept.

I like to start with the project team. These people are not only vital to project success but also can act as ambassadors to other stakeholders, whose services may be equally vital. I particularly have in mind the general operational services of an organisation, whose speed and quality of service to a project may have to be better than they provide on a business-as-usual basis. (Refer to Chapter 3 for methods of harnessing the services of operational groups.)

I find that a few well-chosen examples of quality, presented to the team at a short meeting, will help to demonstrate the concept. The following is an approach that works well.

Give each team member three sheets of A4 paper. These should comprise:

  i) a low-cost 80 gsm sheet of white copier paper
 ii) a high-cost 100 gsm sheet of brilliant white wove paper, with watermark
iii) a sheet of 160 gsm white card.

Ask each team member to rate each sheet in order of quality and their reasons for rating. Rate 1 to 5, with 5 being the highest rating. Record the ratings on a white board or flipchart. The majority of members will rate the brilliant white wove as the highest quality, and the copier paper as the lowest. This reflects a tendency to view quality as meaning 'luxury' or 'high cost'. Some, however, may rate them differently. However, their reasons for rating will reveal whether they have rated quality as meaning luxury.

Some members of the group may want to know what the paper will be used for – an intelligent question, since their choice will depend on usage. Tell these members that they need to make a judgement at this stage just on whether they think the paper is high or low quality.

Next, tell each member that they are to use one of their sheets of paper to construct a three-dimensional paper cat; but first, they need to forecast which type of paper they think would be the most suitable. (Instructions for creating the cat may be found in Appendix A.)

Record the answers, as before. This tests quality as meaning 'fitness for purpose'. Most will probably choose the copier paper, since this seems to have the flexibility needed to make paper folds easily. Few will choose the card, thinking that they might run into trouble when trying to form the smaller folds towards the end of the construction. Some may also notice that the last stage involves blowing into the folds to form the finished cat. They may feel that the card would be just too rigid to unravel the folds into the cat shape. Those using the brilliant white wove will fare better than those using the copier paper, but those using the card will be the most successful, since the rigidity of the card allows softer fold lines to be constructed, allowing easier inflation. Who would have thought it at the beginning?

This demonstrates that quality has to be clearly set in the context of the project deliverables and that the definition of quality cannot always be accomplished from a first impression. Research into the deliverable components and purpose is usually needed in order to select the right quality level.

The demonstration reveals other quality characteristics. For example, how clear were the instructions for constructing the paper cat? Did everyone interpret them in the same way? What skills were needed for the work? Could the work have been better accomplished in a team, with work divided? Quality is as much about efficiency as it is about fitness for purpose. These and other questions are relevant to the definition of quality for a project, as shown in Chapter 2.

I normally run this demonstration for a group of at least ten people. Few manage to complete the task. Some read the instructions but ignore the diagrams, and vice versa. Some do not have the dexterity to make the folds. Most have never done this sort of construction before. The problem is that if a group is not able to follow instructions successfully for creating a paper cat, then how can a project team expect users to operate a new computer system, for example? The demonstration shows that even in a group of ten people, abilities and perceptions are so varied that significant effort is needed to establish consistency.

I sometimes vary the demonstration. I divide the group into three sub-groups. I take one sub-group aside and show them physically, without any instructions, how to construct the cat. When I am confident they have learned the construction, I ask them to write out instructions and diagrams for one of the other sub-groups to use in constructing the cat. I ask the remaining sub-group to assemble the cat using the standard instructions in Appendix A. These latter instructions have been usability-tested; although, as you know in this world, nothing is ever perfect!

The first sub-group act as observers. How well are the second sub-group able to interpret their instructions? Are the third sub-group faring any better with the usability-tested instructions?

This demonstrates that writing instructions for others is quite difficult. Writers must somehow forget their existing knowledge and write for an audience who must be assumed to have zero knowledge of the product. It has been said that some newspapers used to assume an audience with a reading age of eight! Maybe not so much now, but if you want your audience to understand you, you need to write at their level of comprehension.

Quality maxims

In the table opposite I commend nine quality maxims, any one of which would have an effect on a business that lacks any overt quality adoption currently. Each of these maxims is reviewed throughout this book.

Summary

Quality is a perception. It is not absolute but relative to each person's viewpoint and experience. In business, quality is commonly defined as 'fitness for purpose', but 'meeting or

Maxim	Where reviewed
Commit to quality *A commitment to quality from the top of a company or organisation, demonstrated by rewards for quality work and improvement suggestions and the adoption of an overall quality standard, such as ISO 9000*	Ch. 1
Invest in quality *An investment in quality by a company or organisation, demonstrated by regular training and education in quality for staff*	Ch. 1
Adopt a quality mindset *Encouragement for staff to think about and practise quality management in everything they do*	Ch. 1
Quality is everybody's responsibility *Quality is not just the remit of a few persons. Individuals need to assume a responsibility for a complete process, not just their piece*	Ch. 4, 9
Utilise lessons learned and manage knowledge *Provisions for storing and retrieving past project experiences*	Ch. 5
Avoid rework *Practise good planning to get it right first time*	Ch. 5
Practise re-use *The provision of templates based on experience, for consistency and fast application*	Ch. 5
Focus on customer satisfaction *Measuring customer satisfaction and adopting win-win strategies*	Ch. 2
Be prepared *Quality comes from preparation*	Ch. 2

exceeding expectations and requirements' and 'customer satisfaction' are also expressions of quality. Quality is not an isolated activity within a project, but part and parcel of the whole project environment.

The risks of not attending to quality are many, but frequently manifest themselves as delays to benefits accrual, increased costs and time. When external pressures are brought to bear on a project quality can be one of the casualties. The cost of quality can be measured against the risk of project failure.

The most effective companies and organisations are those whose personnel have adopted a quality mindset. Quality has to be sponsored from the top of an organisation, however. It will not evolve by default.

2

Quality definition

The process of quality definition is the first and most important quality task to be achieved in a project or programme. Adopting a formal quality definition process is well worth doing, whatever the end deliverables specified for a project, since it can pay dividends later in terms of reducing disagreements between parties.

Quality definition needs to be undertaken as soon as requirements start to become available from stakeholders. It can be an incremental process, run in parallel with the activity of agreeing the project requirements, or it can be a series of workshops that are run once sets of requirements have been agreed. Experience shows, however, that the process of defining quality for agreed requirements can frequently cause a re-think of those requirements.

Defining the stakeholders is often an exercise in its own right. Although it might be clear who the prime stakeholder is, there may be others who will believe they need a say in the project's requirements and, therefore, its quality. (See the section 'Identifying the stakeholders' in this chapter.) The most important requirement is to gain *common understanding* of the desired quality. Otherwise, the project will be continually dogged by changes and re-directions.

For projects, quality needs to be considered within two key focus areas: *the project deliverables* and *the project management approach* (method, system) employed to manage the work. Although each of these areas is influenced by various factors, it is important to note that the project deliverables are themselves

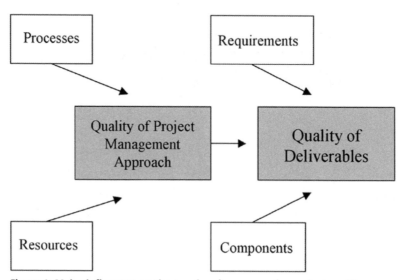

Figure 1: Major influences on the two key focus areas for project quality

considerably influenced by the project management approach. Figure 1 sums this up.

Checking requirements

Quality can only be set if requirements are discussed and agreed with stakeholders before work commences. Thereafter, a regular checking of expectations will ensure that everything continues to conform to requirements.

What does the word 'requirements' really mean, though? Figure 2 shows typical top levels of a requirements breakdown structure (RBS). Here you can see that requirements are not just the wishes of various types of stakeholder but include aspects such as conformance to legislation and standards. Requirements are not only confined to the hard deliverables, either, but also include the requirements for managing the project itself.

I recommend the construction of an RBS as the first stage in quality definition, since it will show the scale of requirements against which quality needs to be applied. There always seems to be a surprise at the variety and number of stakeholders, for example. Similarly, in a construction project, the number of legislative requirements (local authority building regulations, electrical safety regulations, etc.) is usually extensive.

The RBS is a good way of gaining agreement and commitment to the scope of requirements. Initial construction of an RBS for a particular project type can be a lengthy process, but for future,

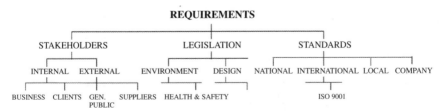

Figure 2: Typical top levels of a requirements breakdown structure

similar projects it may be re-used. Re-use is, of course, a standard quality goal.

For many projects, requirements sign-off is a protracted affair. Certainly, much depends on having formal agreement to requirements. The change control process, for example, cannot be switched on if requirements have not been pinned down. Also, although the quality definition process can be commenced based on assumptions, it cannot be completed.

There is enormous temptation to proceed with a project without requirements sign-off, but the risks of doing so need to be well understood. These include the risks of additional effort and, therefore, cost, resulting from changes to work already commenced. If suppliers are involved, these costs and delays can be significant, since a project does not have direct control of third party schedules. Morale can also be affected if a development environment is particularly unstable.

When checking requirements, a project manager must answer several questions:

1. Are the requirements well articulated and comprehensible?
2. Are they specific or vague?
3. Are they accurate?
4. Are they feasible?
5. Can it be proven when they are satisfied?

The first question checks to see whether the requirements have been clearly and unambiguously stated. Requirements need to be stated in a way that avoids any double meaning, and so reduces the risk of misinterpretation. Unclear requirements are commonly one of the biggest threats to projects. So many project managers take too much for granted with respect to requirements. If a project manager cannot understand a requirement, it is not a valid excuse to believe that someone else must be able to do so. A project manager in this situation must demand an interpretation, since he is accountable for ensuring the requirements are met. What is certain is that unclear requirements will cause significant problems for a project at some stage.

The crucial point comes when a change needs to be made. I have experienced many client arguments about the interpretation of requirements and heard numerous reasons why a client should not be billed for changes that need to be made because of misunderstood statements in the requirements.

The second question concerns the detail of the requirements. How specifically stated are the requirements means how well someone can organise them into a work package. For example, in a roll-out project, have all the user locations and quantities of users been specified? Question three adds the question of accuracy to this. Are the figures mentioned in the requirements accurate? Invitations to tender are notorious for not specifying complete or accurate requirements, so considerable verification often has to be undertaken.

Question four checks whether the requirements can actually be achieved. It is a commonly relevant question in IT projects, where requirements can be increasingly innovative. Additional questions can be asked, such as: How novel are the requirements? Have they ever been addressed before? What research or prior testing has been carried out? Similarly, in construction projects, new materials may be specified or the construction may be being undertaken for the first time in a specific environment. Requirements need to be matched against functional components. The construction of a *House of Quality* is a useful technique for showing this relationship. See Figure 15 in Chapter 6 for details of this approach.

The fifth question checks for evidence that the requirements can be signed off. In other words, can the requirements be

Requirement	Stakeholder	Interest
R17 *Regionally based end-user training for 750 staff*	Business operations Director	Sponsor
	37 x Branch office managers	Local operational management
	Office supervisors	LO supervisory
	Staff	Local operational
	Regional training mgr	Training
R18 *Training Manual for BO Staff*	37 x Branch office managers	Local operational management
	Office supervisors	LO supervisory
	Staff	Local operational
	Help desk staff	Support
	ABC Consultancy	Manual production
	Regional training mgr	Training

Table 2: Sample requirements stakeholder grid

measurable, so that it will be obvious when they have been satisfied? There is a strong link here to success and acceptance criteria, which are key quality requirements.

Matching requirements to stakeholders is an important exercise, which can be verified during a *quality definition workshop* (see section later in this Chapter). A simple grid can be constructed to show which stakeholders have either a direct or indirect stake in a particular requirement. Table 2 shows an example. The grid can form a useful component of the communication plan.

The quality definition process

The quality definition process comprises several important

definition steps. What should be accomplished first is an agreement on the quality viewpoint. For example, will the end-users' view of quality be prevalent, or will it be that of the product developers or the executive management, or a combination of all? Perhaps many groups will want a say in the definition of quality.

Of course, any definition of quality needs to be set according to where quality can be found in the project, and where it can be measured. For example, within the *project deliverables* focus area it is possible to have:

- a quality product
  in terms of defect-free components, thoroughly tested to agreed standards by developers and users
- quality marketing
  to sell the concept of the idea and end-product
- quality training
  that meets audience needs and capabilities, etc.
- quality documentation
  in terms of products, training and user manuals, which are both readable and usable
- quality support
  to provide an adequately staffed and trained help desk, for example.

Within the *project management approach* focus area, it is possible to have:

- quality communication
  to thoroughly set company and user expectations of what will be implemented
- quality planning
  providing for a properly planned and organised project

- quality estimates of costs and benefits
  which use proven techniques to make reliable assessments
- quality resources
  which have the skills to deliver the product solution
- quality implementation
  with fully documented definitions of procedure, responsibilities, etc.

In all of the above examples, the level of desired quality can be set and achieved. Notice how the back end (project deliverables) is heavily reliant on the quality applied to its front-end contributors (project management). It is analogous to decorating a room of a house. All the work is in the front-end preparation. The more diligent this is, the better will be the end result.

Figure 3 shows typical quality activities across a generic project's lifespan. It is clear that quality definition and requirements agreement trigger the remaining activities.

A good approach is to look along the project time-lines, and search out the areas where quality will matter. Then, for each focus

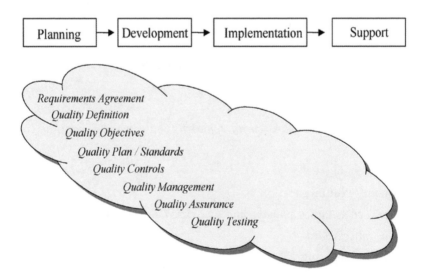

Figure 3: Opportunities for tackling quality across a generic project lifespan

area, understand what things will dictate the level of quality required (the *quality drivers*).

For example, a typical quality driver for end-user documentation might be staff turnover. A high staff turnover would demand a particular level of quality commensurate with a high documentation usage. Comparisons would need to be made with training and support quality levels, since all three will affect the end benefit.

Typical questions to ask are:

- How often will the documentation be used?
- Is it a substitute for training or 1st or 2nd level support?
- In what environment will it be used?
- At what skill level is it aimed?

These are effectively *quality considerations*. They relate to one or more quality drivers and form the link between quality drivers and *quality objectives*, which are the end statements of quality for a project's deliverables and management process.

The definition process is complete when quality objectives have been finalised. These should be aligned to the project objectives, and, in all cases, should be quantifiable. The quality drivers can form the basis of the objectives, so the task of setting objectives need not be arduous. A prime aim of the objectives is to ensure common understanding among the project team. Agreed objectives will be a foundation for managing quality throughout the life of the project.

A good way to do this visually is to produce a *quality definition map*. The mapping of quality drivers to quality objectives may be accomplished using soft systems methodology (SSM). Pathways from drivers to objectives may be shown, together with dependencies. The map is best produced during a *quality definition*

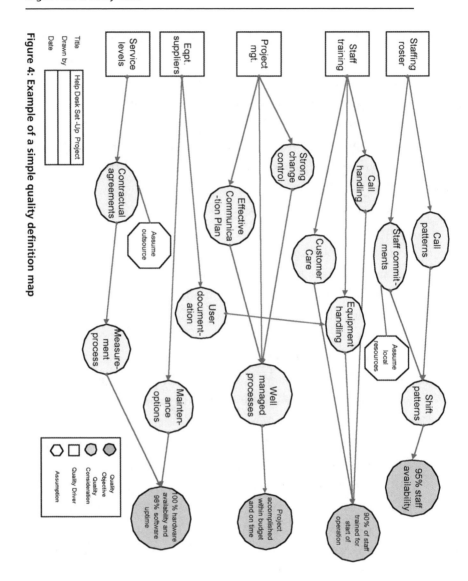

Figure 4: Example of a simple quality definition map

workshop (see below), when all principal stakeholders can contribute and agree the picture.

Figure 4 shows an example of a quality definition map for a help desk set-up project, produced using SSM principles. This is a simple example, showing you what can be achieved through relating quality drivers to quality objectives. Note that in this example the map is for the project to set up the help desk and not for the help desk function. The quality objectives for a steady-state operation would be different. For example, '95% of calls answered within 30 seconds'.

The map can show the number of contributing pathways towards the quality objectives. It also shows the focus points for quality (quality considerations). Some of these can become key nodes, if several pathways lead into them.

Identifying the stakeholders

What is a project stakeholder? Essentially, a project stakeholder is someone who has a stake or interest in a project. This may be a vested interest, through a personal investment or sponsorship. It may be accountability for part of the action – for example, someone who has something to build, manage or support. A stakeholder is certainly likely to be someone or a group of people who will receive the results of the project.

A project can have many stakeholders – some obvious, some less obvious. A programme is likely to have even more. These stakeholders will each have varying degrees of influence on the project. Some may be direct investors, some may be members of a user community, and some may be suppliers and maintainers. Some may be internal to a company; others may be external in the public domain.

An important initial quality task is to identify all the stakeholders and their requirements. Their requirements may not be obvious.

25

Many may be hidden and only come to light once significant work on the project has been done. Assumptions need to be made for all types of stakeholder, and then tested for expectations. Stakeholder identification is an important input into the project communication plan; because once stakeholders have been identified they need to be kept in communication with the project.

I find it best to construct a map of the stakeholders: who they are and how they relate to the project in a cultural sense. The map is best constructed through an initial survey. Assumptions can be made by the project team about who the stakeholders might be. The detailed information can be collected through interviews with each stakeholder or stakeholder group. Figure 5 shows the sort of information that I like to collect. It shows the influence or

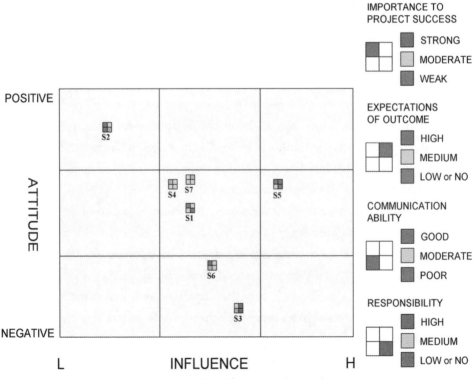

Figure 5: Map of stakeholders by influence and attitude

power that a stakeholder might wield, plotted against a perception of their attitude to the project. In others words, how important are they likely to be to the success of the project and are they likely to support the project in a positive way or to cause trouble?

Four ratings are made with respect to these axes: importance to project success; expectations of outcome; communication ability; responsibility. For example, one would expect the project sponsor to be strongly in favour of project success, with high expectations of outcome and is likely to be a person of senior responsibility. The Sponsor, however, might be a poor communicator, so score low in communication ability. It is important to know communication ability for stakeholders, since good expectation setting will be influenced by the method of communication. It is no good sending someone lots of emails if they never read them or respond to them.

The choice of a fourfold rating can be made according to the type of project. Other rating considerations might be just as appropriate. I would advise you to retain the communication ability, though, for the reasons mentioned above.

I feel I must issue a health warning with this type of map. It could be political dynamite! I would not advise sharing the map widely, since it represents personal opinions by the project team and there may well be stakeholders who would disagree with the perceptions made. Its contained use, however, is beneficial. Much time can be saved through fully understanding who is voting for your project and who is less enthusiastic about its outcome.

CTQ

As I stated in the Introduction, there are many who believe that quality is free. This may be true in terms of attitude. Having a quality attitude costs nothing. However, training your staff to develop a quality attitude costs money. Striving overtly to attain

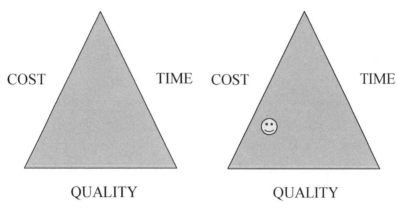

Figure 6: The cost, time, quality triangle   Figure 7: Relative positioning of CTQ

quality also takes time and, therefore, costs money. Due diligence, for example, takes longer to achieve than unconsidered work.

Figure 6 shows the Cost, Time, Quality Triangle (CTQ). The desirable outcome for any project is regularly voiced as 'successful to cost, time and quality'. If you try to place your project as a dot within the triangle against the three attributes of cost, time and quality you will find that you cannot have all three attributes except in equal proportions. This is because, in practice, they are conflicting attributes. Squeeze one of them and you tend to affect the others. When the pressure is on, however, the easiest to relinquish is quality, since businesses feel that cost and time are usually too visible to relinquish lightly. The consideration of time, cost and quality for projects is, therefore, always a trade-off.

Cost and time seem much more definite attributes than quality. Many perceive quality as a rather vague, loosely defined thing – not unlike how they might perceive risk, in fact. It is often difficult to grasp in concept or perceive in practice. Not surprisingly, projects are frequently delivered without any specific measurements of quality or quality success criteria.

The attributes of cost, time and quality are, therefore, uneven in their perception. So much so, that *scope* or *performance* has often been substituted for quality in the CTQ triangle. However, just because perception may be difficult, I don't believe it justifies making quality a poor relation. Scope and performance are, anyway, absolutes, not attributes, so entirely inappropriate for components of the CTQ triangle.

Nonetheless, the CTQ triangle has a use, and that is to focus the minds of stakeholders on what will be predominant for a particular project. Will cost, time or quality be the main focus? The answer is important to a project manager, since it will have a bearing on the deployment of effort, budget and resources. In Figure 7, the position of the smiley face reveals that Cost is the most important attribute, Quality is also important, but Time is of little importance.

Keeping the attributes in balance is an important task for a project manager. He should be regularly checking for any changes to stakeholder perceptions of CTQ through the normal execution of the communication plan.

There is often much discussion regarding the cost of quality. The Introduction to this book gives several examples of where attention to quality can prevent future effort and, therefore, reduce costs. How much attention is given to this by a project is part of the balancing requirement, mentioned above. A product launched with poor quality will result in increased support costs, for example.

I find it useful to employ the *decision tree* technique when needing to make a decision on whether to increase time or cost against quality. Figure 8 (overleaf) shows an example constructed mid-way in the development of a new mobile phone product. It seeks to answer the question whether to curtail testing and launch the product in order to beat heavy competition to the marketplace or whether to increase testing time and launch a more robust product. This is a typical dilemma for many projects, when faced with mounting pressures. The decision tree in this example indicates that the risk exposure is less when the extended

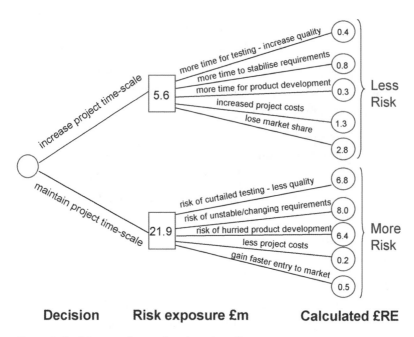

Decision **Risk exposure £m** **Calculated £RE**

Figure 8: Decision tree for product launch options

testing option is taken. In other words, the expected value is more favourable.

The quality definition workshop

The best way to define quality is via a group session of stakeholders. Running a quality definition workshop (QDW) is an excellent way of gaining buy-in to the quality management process. The workshop should be run during project start-up, ideally when requirements have been identified. It can also be run during any contract bidding stage, but would need to be re-run following any successful bid.

The principal aim is to obtain a definition of the level of quality for all aspects of a project. This includes not only deliverables but also how the project will be resourced and managed. In the following procedure for a QDW, a quality definition map is constructed as an overall quality baseline for the project. (Refer to Figure 4, page 24, for an example of this.)

Scope and boundaries

The QDW can be run as a half-day, day or two-day session. Any less time than a half-day is likely to be unproductive; any more time than two days is likely to be too cumbersome for the participants. However, it depends on the nature and size of the project and also on how importantly quality is perceived for the project (viz. CTQ). Certainly, the workshop should start with an assessment of CTQ. If quality proves not to be a significant attribute for the project, then quality definition might better be undertaken within an overall project definition session, rather than at a specific workshop for quality definition.

Input material

It will be useful if the project team has produced a stakeholder map. Stakeholders should at least have been identified.

The most important inputs to the workshop are the statements of requirements and deliverables. The current project plan is also important. It is possible to prioritise the tasks on the plan and merely assess the most critical of these at the workshop. Other useful material might be contracts, statements of work, the project work breakdown structure and organisation breakdown structure, lists of dependencies and assumptions, risk and issue logs.

It is important to circulate project material in advance of the workshop. QDW relies heavily on clear perceptions and assumptions. Participants need to come to the workshop prepared and ready to engage in significant debate.

Participants

Participants for the workshop should be the core project team, key stakeholders plus other interested parties who are able to add value to the exercise. These might be client representatives, subcontractors (working both externally and internally), various business functional representatives and the project sponsor, for example. It may not be possible to obtain a full team, but the more diverse the participants, the better the coverage will be.

An experienced facilitator will be required. This should not be the project manager. He or she will need the freedom to participate. A note-taker will be useful as much of the ensuing debate could be useful for later analysis.

Agenda

The agenda can be fairly open within the overall time allowed. Table 3 summarises the key steps. It is useful for the project manager to give an introduction and state the background to the project. Some of the participants may be meeting for the first time, so this is a great opportunity for team-building.

Deciding the focus areas can be next on the agenda. The sub-projects, phases and divisions of the project can be a useful guide. It will probably be necessary to prioritise the focus areas in order to accommodate discussion within the time allowed for the workshop. Within the focus areas, the deliverables and requirements then need to be assessed. How complete are these?

Agenda item	Responsibility
Welcome and project background	Project manager
The project in a business context	Project sponsor
Introduction to the workshop process	Facilitator
Identification of focus areas	All, lead by facilitator
Identification of quality objectives	All, lead by facilitator
Identification of quality drivers	All, lead by facilitator
Identification of quality considerations	All, lead by facilitator
Agreement to the draft quality definition map	All, lead by facilitator
Wrap-up and next steps	Project manager

Table 3: Suggested agenda for quality definition workshop

The questions asked in *Checking requirements* at the start of this chapter also need to be verified. Requirements need to be matched against stakeholders. Here there may be a one to many relationship. It is important to know, however, which stakeholders are interested in which requirements, either directly or indirectly.

Once the requirements and deliverables have been assessed, the quality objectives need to be agreed in outline. (Refer to the section entitled *Quality objectives* later in this chapter.) These should be quantified and relate to specific deliverables. This activity can be accomplished to good effect by getting participants to write their suggestions and the focus area to which they apply, on sticky notes, which can be arranged on a white board. The activity should not be laboured. If participants experience difficulty, proceeding to the next step might help – identification of the *quality drivers*.

The quality drivers are those aspects or situations that drive the definition of quality for a particular project. Figure 4 shows some examples. They can be specific or non-specific.

With the quality drivers suitably arranged, participants can then suggest *quality considerations*. These are literally what they indicate – the opportunities for quality within specific deliverables. (Refer to the section in this chapter, *Reaching consensus*, for a method of deciding how they should be defined.) The quality considerations can be arranged as a flow extending from the quality drivers and leading to the quality objectives.

The quality considerations are then linked to either further quality considerations or direct to the quality objectives. It should then be possible to look again at the quality objectives, particularly if any difficulty was encountered initially.

Finally, the pathways are checked on the map and the quality objectives verified.

Output

The output of the QDW is a draft quality definition map and a list of quantified quality objectives, plus a firm commitment to building the results into the master project plan. Refinement of the quality definition map is likely, so provision should be made to schedule any further meetings required.

All the decisions made should be input to the project Quality Plan (see Chapter 5).

Reaching consensus

One of the most difficult things to achieve in the quality definition process is overall consensus. It is difficult, not only because of the fact that quality is a perception, but also because quality is often difficult to describe adequately. It is something that is frequently visible and understandable in hindsight, particularly in terms of cost, effort and benefit. During quality definition, though, it is often an act of faith for the stakeholders involved.

Stakeholders often do not know the quality considerations for their requirements. They may not even have given quality much thought. In this case, the project team must help them decide, taking them through the various options for establishing quality.

Projects have failed because stakeholders failed to reach agreement on goals or requirements, and continued to disagree during project execution. (See the Bremen Space Centre example in Chapter 3.) Agreement sometimes requires considerable diplomacy; and a project manager must decide how much variation exists against how much effort is needed to bridge any gaps.

Some programmes with multiple stakeholders actively implement a marketing campaign to sell the benefits well before work commences. This tests for any out-of-line views or differing expectations. It also prevents the situation where stakeholders meet for the first time after the project has

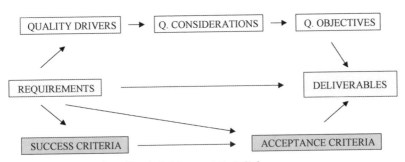

Figure 9: Aspects of quality definition and their links

commenced and find that they have not had any prior opportunity to give their input.

I remember a company bidding for the delivery of IT systems to the public sector, which was specifically banned from contacting the user stakeholders until after the award of the contract. Not surprisingly, there were several surprises in terms of 'real' requirements that emerged when the company finally got to meet the stakeholders.

In terms of reaching consensus, therefore, the principal maxim must be that the more time and effort is put into understanding the expectations and requirements of the various stakeholders prior to project start-up, the less problematic in terms of conflicts will be the later stages of the project.

Figure 9 shows all the quality definition aspects that need to be agreed. It shows how they are linked and the sequence of definition. For example, quality objectives cannot be decided until quality considerations have been defined. The Figure shows that it is possible, of course, to go straight from requirements into the construction of deliverables without any considerations of quality.

Figure 9 is a good way of providing a simple explanation to stakeholders of the quality definition process. It demonstrates that both success criteria and acceptance criteria are aspects of quality and not stand-alone considerations.

Deliverables

Project deliverables are towards the end of the quality pathway and provide the tangible evidence of the quality effort that has gone before. It is not within the scope of this book to give guidance on the production of deliverables; instead I want to demonstrate their important quality aspects and considerations.

As can be seen from Figure 1, deliverables are made up of components. These may be hard components, such as machine parts, or soft components, such as a set of online business forms. Some project management methodologies refer to deliverables as products, which certainly reflects the construction that needs to go into producing them. However, with all products, there is often a tendency to ignore the familiar and take for granted that many of the components are trustworthy and will, therefore, work. This is somewhat similar to requirements.

Products are often assumed to operate correctly, although they may only been tested once in the past. However, we know that situations and environments change, such that a product working well in one environment may not do so in another. The maxim is, therefore, take nothing for granted. A good project manager will always test a product for a particular situation.

Customers for a company's products will expect them to work in their environments. I am reminded of a cash dispensing machine that refused to operate correctly in a retail fast-food outlet, even though it had been thoroughly tested at the factory. The problem only came to light through detailed observation of the local operation. The shop manager regularly had greasy hands and replenished the cash in the machine without washing them. The odd, greasy note was prone to jamming in the machine. Usability testing could possibly detect this sort of thing, but the real message is to avoid errors by assessing the situations in which deliverables will be used.

At the start of a project, requirements need to be interpreted as specific deliverables. This can be as protracted an undertaking as reaching agreement on the requirements themselves. It will certainly be reflected in how well the answers were made to the questions in the *Checking requirements* section, above. From a quality perspective, the pathway from requirements to deliverables is especially important, since the human elements involved feature strongly. These latter comprise *making perceptions, having expectations, making assumptions* and *reaching agreements* – all notoriously complex and difficult.

The tangible deliverables are by and large relatively simple to articulate and demonstrate, compared to the intangible deliverables. In all cases, though, it is time that reveals whether deliverables are truly accepted by an organisation or not. So, how far should a project team go regarding acceptance of a deliverable? Acceptance is, after all, a key quality consideration.

The problem needs to be faced, since history is full of projects that delivered working solutions, which later failed during extensive use. Business operations and circumstances change regularly. So does technology. One could say that the project should not be accountable for success beyond certain limits of time or tolerances. It is quite possible, and recommended from a quality perspective, that agreement be reached on these limits.

Softer deliverables, such as new business processes or changes to existing processes, will only prove themselves over time. A good project manager will check with the relevant business analysts to satisfy himself that due diligence has been done with regard to a project that delivers a business process. In my experience such investigations can be quite revealing, particularly where an existing process is changed. The question is, how responsible should a project manager feel if a delivered business process fails to work as expected? I feel that a project manager should at least exercise due diligence by asking searching questions about a process to be delivered: Why is it being changed? How will it be different? What studies have been done? Has the process been studied end-to-end? Who else has implemented the process, with what results?

In a programme, there is a built-in ability to see the progress of implemented deliverables. As each project completes, the programme itself continues, and with it the ability to monitor the effectiveness of implemented deliverables through the programme and make any corrective action required. A roll-out project to multiple sites has a similar, though lesser, monitoring ability. Initial implementations to sites will show whether generic problems in deliverables take-up will occur, thus allowing corrective action to be taken for later implementations.

Quality is as much about the management of the project as the deliverables. If a building falls down, but the project manager has followed the architect's plans and exercised due diligence, then the architect is accountable. If, however, the project manager has blindly followed the plans without questioning and failed to raise concerns, then the project manager must also be accountable.

I remember a company that sought to shorten a product ordering process by cutting out a process step, in order to reduce the order lead-time and save resource costs. This was done, however, without any full analysis of the end-to-end process. The results were disastrous, since not only was a resource removed, but also a skill. The resource upstream of the removed resource did not have the skill to fill the gap. The damage to the company's image through frustrated customers was significant. In this instance, the project manager failed to ask even the most basic questions above regarding the changed process and merely took for granted that the new process would work.

The project Quality Plan, outlined in Chapter 5, should record all the deliverables and their components. In particular, it should record their origin, by whom and how they will be constructed, where they fit in to the overall solution, by whom and how they will be tested, and by whom and how they will be accepted. A configuration management plan may be necessary to keep track of certain deliverables (refer to Chapter 6).

Quality considerations

Quality considerations relate directly to stakeholder requirements, though they are often born out of considering quality drivers. Essentially, they are the things that need to be considered when defining quality objectives. This means that they are on the pathway from requirements to quality objectives, as shown in Figure 9. Although, therefore, they may be seen as only a stepping stone on the road to quality definition, they are a very important one.

The best way to decide quality considerations is against some relevant criteria for your particular project and/or organisation. It is possible, however, to define some fairly generic criteria, which would be applicable to most deliverables. Table 4 (overleaf) gives some examples, breaking out quality considerations into categories and sub-categories. Some aspects may be common to more than one category, such as cost.

Do not forget the question of support for deliverables. Support is not just a cost factor over the lifetime of a deliverable, but whether the quality factors will be durable. I often admire the Albert Bridge in London at night, with its hundreds of light bulbs illuminated across the spans. The row of lights is never complete, however. There are always some missing, spoiling the continuous line. I wonder whether this maintenance effort was ever fully considered, when someone decided, on aesthetic grounds, how nice it would be to have the bridge illuminated in this way!

If you think defining the quality considerations for your project is arduous, bear in mind that with each similar project, the

Category	Sub-Category 1	Sub-Category 2
Technical	Limitations	Design limits
		Technical boundaries / possibilities
		Limits to availability of equipment or components
		Cost limitations
	Maintainability	
Regulatory	Standards	
	Statutory requirements	Tolerances
		Statutory limitations
		Environmental
Company	Standards	
	Policy	Budget constraints
Manpower	Staff head-count	
	Skills availability	
Aesthetic	Design	Design limitations
		Attractive and functional
		Award winning
Support	Geographic coverage	

Table 4: Some generic categories for quality considerations, applicable to deliverables

identification of quality considerations becomes easier, assuming the knowledge gained has been stored for later retrieval. Using lessons learned from previous projects is itself a sound quality principle.

Defined quality considerations should be used to compose the quality objectives (see below), and it is these latter that should appear in the project Quality Plan.

Success criteria

Success criteria indicate whether a project has been successfully managed and successfully implemented, and usually take the form of written statements that answer the question: *What does success look like in relation to this project?* Success criteria are also known as critical success factors.

In envisaging success, it is useful to employ the technique of *backcasting*[1]. This is simply imagining a final result that is successful and working back to try and understand what activities led to this state. It is, therefore, different from merely forecasting the end result. Backcasting selects a picture of success and allows a pathway to be built from the present towards that goal. It asks questions such as 'What events happened just before we achieved success?' and 'What events occurred just before these?' Extrapolating back from success is a creative exercise that helps a project team set interim goals, the achievement of which are measurable. So many projects concentrate on failure, looking regularly at the things that could go wrong. Regrettably, risk management can foster this by focusing on the negative. Good risk management, of course, focuses on the opportunities as well as the threats.

Success in project terms relates not just to the implementation of deliverables, but also to how the project was managed. The performance of the project team, efficient use of skills, costs and expenses, are important requirements for many stakeholders.

Certain deliverables are less obvious than others in how they will look and operate following construction. In IT projects, for example, it is often quite difficult to conceive the final solution from the requirements specification stage. Even when building something tangible, such as a house, the end product may not be exactly as envisaged. However, it may still be deemed 'fit for purpose' and, therefore, thought of as a success.

Specifying success criteria in advance enables a project to focus its objectives. The question in this context for a project manager is always: 'How will I know that I have been successful with this project?'. Success criteria attempt to answer this question, so that

---

1 Isochron Ltd (www.isochron.co.uk)

Project objectives	Success criteria
Deliver a business process for dealing with customer complaints to all UK regions	Customer service (CS) staff will be able to operate the customer complaints process seamlessly within the context of the overall CS business, from delivery All CS staff will be trained in the new process from delivery
Provide a support capability for the customer complaints process	Support processes will be operational at delivery, with a response time of better than 2 minutes
Deliver the project by September 30th, using existing CS resources	No additional cost for resources – existing CS head count only deployed

Table 5: Example of some project success criteria in relation to project objectives

a project manager knows whether he is on the right track towards achieving the project objectives. To this latter end, it may sometimes be convenient to specify phased success criteria. A project manager will then have a measurement of success to apply at the end of, say, Stage 1. This is a common approach employed in complex programmes, where, typically, the end of the programme is not clearly detailed.

The link from success criteria to project or programme objectives is, therefore, important. The criteria should always be measurable and support the measurable objectives of the project. Table 5 gives some examples. Note that the project objectives do not specify quality aspects, since these will be covered in the quality objectives. Success criteria, however, may refer to aspects of quality when describing what success will look like.

Acceptance criteria

There is sometimes confusion over the difference between success criteria and acceptance criteria. There is certainly a close link, and the two terms are occasionally used interchangeably. Essentially, acceptance criteria specify the conditions of acceptance for a project's intended purpose rather than whether a project has been deemed an overall success. Broadly speaking, acceptance criteria relate to specific deliverables and success criteria relate to the project as a whole.

Because success criteria are expressions of overall project requirement, it is feasible to decide them before acceptance criteria. Figure 9, therefore, shows success criteria leading into acceptance criteria.

Both acceptance criteria and success criteria have a strong link to testing, since they both relate to proof of quality. The output of any testing is usually an acceptance or sign-off. Acceptance criteria should provide the measurement for this.

Acceptance criteria are often cited in contracts. Invitations to tender may require the specification of acceptance criteria. Payment may be withheld unless the criteria can be shown to have been met. This is often a problematic situation for projects, particularly if the criteria have not been specified clearly or to a fine level of detail. I have witnessed many arguments concerning the interpretation of acceptance criteria at a critical point in time. This critical point usually relates to an impending payment period.

Table 6 shows some examples of acceptance criteria. Notice how much more detailed they are than the success criteria in Table 5.

Project	Deliverable	Acceptance criteria
Customer complaints process	Customer validation check	The customer validation check must be completable online within 30 seconds, from data input to displayed result
	Customer response	The process should allow a response to a written customer complaint to be accomplished within 2 working days

Table 6: Some examples of acceptance criteria for specific deliverables

The specification of acceptance criteria should not be a laborious activity. Bearing in mind that the purpose of acceptance criteria is to provide guidance for evidence that shows a deliverable can be signed off as acceptable, the level of detail should be just sufficient to support this activity. Acceptance criteria will form a useful audit trail. It is not unusual to hear questions such as 'Who signed this off?' or 'Who accepted this?' when things go wrong.

Quality objectives

Quality objectives represent the end statements of quality for a deliverable. They provide the statements that show specifically the desired level of quality. Project objectives, by contrast, tend to state the overall objectives for a project, and not necessarily to deliverable level. Project objectives may contain quality requirements, as well as cost, benefit and time requirements, for example, but it is useful to be able to refer particularly to quality at a deliverable level through the use of quality objectives. This is so that quality control and quality assurance are able to relate directly to specific quality needs.

Table 7 shows some examples of quality objectives for the

Deliverable	Quality objective
Customer validation check	The customer validation check must operate seamlessly within the customer complaints process, ie, no disruption to the process throughput or cycle time
Customer response	The customer response format should be courteously worded and include the ability to select without error the paragraphs specified in document CS/RP1
	The customer response format should allow the selection without ambiguity of responses to all complaint situations listed in document CS/CC1, together with a user definable response for an unlisted situation

Table 7: Some examples of quality objectives for specific deliverables

Heading	Interpretation
Usability	Considering the use of the deliverable, eg, *staff must be able to operate the deliverable without needing a physics degree*
Durability	Considering how robust the deliverable needs to be, eg, *the menu sheets must be constructed using a material that can take regular handling in a fast-food restaurant environment, yet maintain a clean appearance*
Cost	Considering cost or budget constraints for the deliverable, eg, *construction of the deliverable should cost no more than £30 per unit*
Time	Considering the operating cycle for the deliverable, eg, *the cisterns must be fillable within four minutes*
Performance	Considering the performance of the deliverable, eg, *the system should operate error-free for the first six months, thereafter it should not experience down-time of more than 2 minutes per quarter*
Maintenance	Considering all aspects of the support and maintenance of the deliverable, eg, *cost, service level*
Context	Considering how the deliverable will operate in relation to other deliverables, eg, *the process should not disrupt the normal business operation*
Standards	Considering how the deliverable needs to conform to an existing standard, eg, *the documentation must conform to the company security standard*

Table 8: Some generic groupings for quality objectives

deliverables in Table 6. The quality objectives are quite different from the acceptance criteria, although closer in sentiment to the project objectives and project success criteria.

Quality objectives typically fall into a few groups. Table 8 lists some generic groupings for consideration within quality objectives. Some companies and organisations may specify a list of quality headings that must be considered for all deliverables.

Quality objectives should be shown for each deliverable in the Quality Plan. A Quality Plan, however, is a stake in the ground. It is also a living document and represents a baseline against which future changes may be made. So often, quality objectives are reduced or dispensed with when costs become a problem in a project. If quality is made subject to change control as with other project aspects, then the effects of any reduction during a project may be understood. Agreement between stakeholders is, therefore, fundamental.

Quality standards

Many companies and organisations have existing commitments to quality processes. Some will have appointed a quality function with a quality director and quality managers. Some will subscribe to various national or international quality standards, such as BS 6079[2], ISO 9000[3] or Baldridge[4]. It is important for any project being undertaken in such an environment to ensure that the company quality standards are considered. There may well be short-cuts available to a resource-constrained project through being able to utilise existing company quality resources and processes.

It should not be forgotten, however, that a project is operating at a different pace and level from the steady-state business operation and that the project's quality requirements may not be exactly in tune with 'business as usual'.

I recently encountered a good example of this. The standard manufacturing failure rate for a particular component was 5%, but the customer for a special build project desired less than a 2% failure rate. As the standard manufacturing plant was planned to be used for the special build there was thus a conflict in the quality requirement.

It is unlikely that you will need to develop new standards in

---

2 British Standard for project and programme management
3 International Standardisation Organisation standard (see Bibliography for reference)
4 Malcolm Baldrige Award for American business, assessed in seven quality categories

order to undertake a project, though you may embark on a project that is designed to introduce a new standard. Either way, it is not within the scope of this book to provide guidance on the development of standards. For project managers, the need is simply to understand what standards exist so that the project may comply.

In many industries, complying with standards – particularly regulatory standards – can introduce a significant cost factor. It is important, therefore, to be able to understand this before the project budget is set. The building industry is notable in having to comply with new building regulations introduced mid-way in a project. Also, many technology projects come about because of a need to upgrade or replace equipment in order to comply with a new government standard.

The quality objectives and acceptance criteria should incorporate any requirement to conform to a standard.

Summary

Quality definition is a fundamental activity for achieving project quality. If quality cannot be sufficiently and clearly defined then it cannot be adequately built-in to components and deliverables. This also extends to the management system for the project. How a project will be managed and how the team will perform will affect the result of what is being delivered.

The quality definition process should not be curtailed. Sufficient time should be allowed to reach consensus. Moving forward from a firm base will reap the ultimate benefits, saving always much needed time and effort along the way.

3

Setting expectations

Following the definition of quality for a project, the next most important activity is the setting of expectations among all who will be involved with the project. Stakeholder identification should have been done as part of the quality definition activity. This will make it relatively easy to target the required expectation setting activity.

We all have everyday experiences of expectations. They are tested every time we buy something or every time we travel somewhere. We base our expectations on the information we have been given and upon our own past experiences and knowledge. We may arrive at a holiday resort only to find that it is still being constructed. Naturally, we are disappointed. The holiday brochure set our expectations at the time of booking, but someone neglected to tell us of the building work. Consequently, we are disappointed and want to seek redress. We purchase a book that has been recommended by a friend. We read it but are disappointed. Our expectations do not match the recommendation given by our friend. What has happened? We have forgotten that what pleases one person does not necessarily please another.

All this happens in business too, and, particularly in projects. Our expectations are either positive or negative depending on how we perceive a situation. All stakeholders in a project differ in their perceptions and their expectations, so we must ensure that each is addressed accordingly. Those who think that a blanket communication of what will be delivered will be sufficient are deluding themselves. Some will be receptive, but others will not. This is why it is important to *target* stakeholders with regard to expectation setting.

Expectation setting is an ongoing activity and should be carried out ideally as part of the project communication plan. It is the responsibility of the project manager to ensure that this happens, though the activity may be delegated to an experienced communications manager.

Expectation setting is commenced during project start-up and continues throughout the life of a project, when expectations will be set, re-set and continually monitored.

Since deliverable acceptance is based on human perceptions of what will be handed over, expectation setting is of vital importance in assuring project success. How a project's stakeholders will receive information about a project and how they will interpret that information will have a fundamental effect on the acceptance of the project outcome.

Using a communication plan for expectation setting

A common problem for many projects is *faith in the familiar*. I was recently reminded of this when a carpenter, who was building a doorway for me to plans that clearly showed its dimensions and fit-out, failed to meet my requirements. When asked why the doorway was built incorrectly, the carpenter responded: 'But this is how we always build this type of doorway'!

The problem was that the clerk of works had asked the carpenter to build a doorway of a certain type. Because the carpenter was immediately familiar with this type of doorway and had built it hundreds of times before, he neglected to consult the plans, assuming they would match the standard for the familiar type.

Our difficulty is that much of our decision-making is based on the familiar. The need to re-check the familiar and not take it for granted is a warning we must heed. Working on a client site recently, I was warned that the fire alarm would be sounded at 4pm every Monday. When, one Monday, it sounded continuously at 3.45pm I took it for a real threat, but was surprised to see how slowly people evacuated the building. This was not a drill – in fact there had been a small fire in the kitchen. Many, though, assumed the usual practice drill was 15 minutes early and chose to ignore it.

The making of assumptions is part of normal business practice. However, how do you control their validity? In a project context, a project manager needs to find a way to exert a degree of control, since faulty assumptions about what will be delivered will be detrimental to project success. A communication plan, therefore, needs to cater for the obvious and familiar as well as the new.

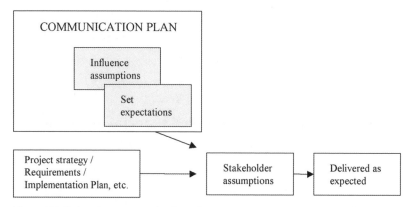

Figure 10: Using the communication plan to promote correct assumptions

Figure 10 shows how a communication plan complements the information that stakeholders receive through the normal planning processes.

The communication plan needs to work alongside the other project management processes. If stakeholder assumptions were to rely solely on technical documents such as a scope of work, requirements plan and overall project plan there is a real risk of misinterpretation of certain pieces of information.

The major focus for project management is now widely accepted to be human interaction rather than technical processes, yet some people still treat a communication plan as a passive document rather than part of an active management approach. This is often because many do not see project communication as a professional activity. 'Well anyone can do it, can't they?' is not an uncommon response.

Part of the communication plan should be the map showing the various project stakeholders and their interest in the project. 'Know your stakeholder' is a key to setting the right expectations. Table 9 shows some typical components of a project communication plan. Although the communication plan is an important project document, I don't feel it should be laboured.

Component	Description
Communication brief	Purpose of the communication plan; management of and resources for the communication plan
Target audience	Who will be affected by the communication plan
Stakeholder list	Description of the project stakeholders, as a specific target audience
Stakeholder map	A plot of stakeholder attitudes and relationships to the project[1]
Stakeholder expectations	Assumptions regarding particular expectations of stakeholders
Communication vehicles	Communication approaches in relation to the various stakeholders and audiences

Table 9: Typical contents of a project communication plan

No one will want to read a weighty volume. Too many project methodologies prescribe 'chapter and verse' for project documentation. I feel, like the contents of this book, that documentation should be sufficient guidance and direction for the activity – a bit like *fitness for purpose*, in fact.

Misconceptions can occur in a project or programme merely through not understanding the meaning of acronyms and terminology. To this end, it is important that the project plan documentation includes a suitable glossary of project terminology. Ambiguity of language can set the wrong expectations.

Assumptions planning is a good route to testing stakeholder expectations. Assumptions give a project team something to test with stakeholders. By making and documenting assumptions, a team can check their validity with stakeholders and have the opportunity to turn them into hard and fast decisions.

The route from perceptions to managed expectations can be summarised as:

---

1 Keep this separate from any publicly available communication plan if the mapped material is politically sensitive.

- perceptions are made by people
- people in projects include stakeholders
- stakeholders have expectations
- expectations can be born from assumptions
- assumptions and expectations both need to be managed.

Reading the stakeholder audience

On a recent project, I and other members of the team became aware that the project support office was up and running, when we started to receive emails bearing statements such as: 'The Risk Management Process is now available and attached. Please start using it immediately.' Each email was accompanied by a 3mb file. As a communication exercise it was, of course, instant death. I couldn't wait for the Communication Process announcement!

Imagine if stakeholders were to receive a similar message: 'Attached are your deliverables. Please let us know if they are correct.' Nice idea, wrong approach.

This all points to the need for professional communication management. Communication requires experience and knowledge of human interaction. To avoid the situation outlined above, for projects of a certain size or criticality, a project manager should seriously consider appointing a professional communications manager to the project team.

A communications manager can manage the rumour mill as much as the communication of the progress of deliverables. Rumours spread quickly in large projects; after all, there is a larger team and more stakeholders in a position to create dialogue. The more personal the subject area, the greater the rumour. For example, I worked on one project where it seemed likely that the premises would quickly become too small and that a move to larger premises would be necessary. Within days, rumours began to build of moves not only within the existing building but also to fairly far flung places. In fact, after a couple of weeks, some rumours were being quoted as certainties and even found their way on to the project issue log!

The importance of ensuring that all stakeholders are brought into the expectations setting process cannot be understated. The project manager may tend to feel less in control of certain groups of stakeholders, as opposed to the project team or direct reports. Nevertheless, a degree of influence needs to be exerted in order to effect buy-in and to generate common understanding of the levels of quality desired.

Stakeholders whose views are not brought into line can prove disastrous to a project. For example, the €600m Space Centre in Bremen, Germany[2], was closed after being open for only 217 days. Not one of the 120 shops in the newly built shopping mall had been let, and attendance at the theme park was well down from forecast figures. Key financial stakeholders were Dresdner Bank and the City of Bremen but these were just at the top of a long list of stakeholders, whose opinions were so diverse that, in the end, none of their expectations was actually met. Size is not a problem, if adequate stakeholder mapping is done and related specifically to a strong communication plan. Even so, balancing the needs for a quick return on investment against philanthropic desires is not easy, and proved to be the downfall of the Space Centre.

In many ways, a project asks a great deal of stakeholders. It assumes that they actually know what they have at present in order to gauge how it will change through the delivery of the project. Of course, any preparatory business analysis should be able to specify what exists in terms of operation or business process. My experience is, though, that many stakeholders are not fully aware of

---

2   26 September 2004. Source: *PM Network*, December 2004

their own 'A' point and so cannot interpret fully the differences between that and the 'B' point. Getting from A to B frequently needs particular explanation, and in a stakeholder's own 'language'.

Two major business changes in recent years tested company knowledge of end-to-end processes: the Year 2000 computing problem and the introduction of the euro. Both these changes revealed a distinct lack of knowledge about even basic processes. Projects and programmes that seek to change business processes, therefore, need to bear this is mind when setting expectations.

Part of this process knowledge is what I call the *quality baseline.* This represents the existing level of quality to be found in any business process or operation that will be changed via a project or programme. Knowing what exists now in terms of quality will help to understand how a project may improve, retain or perhaps lower the existing quality level.

Be aware that the quality baseline applies not just to physical attributes, such as equipment or processes, but also to human perceptions. For example, a worker whose personal desk space is replaced by a hot-desking arrangement as part of a workforce improvement project may have a perception that the quality level of his ability to function at work has lowered. Human resource departments should be able to detect this possibility and tackle it accordingly. However, from a project perspective, the project team would need to be aware that here is a stakeholder who may not be best pleased with the project and so not support it as readily as other types of stakeholders, eg, HR and management.

It is possible to map the quality baseline and include it in the Quality Plan (refer to Chapter 5 for building a Quality Plan).

Testing user mood for change

Projects that deliver softer outcomes, such as business change, are at particular risk of not achieving expectation setting. Here the business case is usually not clear concerning the exact nature of the deliverables. Users may understand that the business may not be the same following implementation of a business change project, but may not understand how what they do today may relate to the new environment.

Projects that introduce new software sometimes have an element of 'no gain without pain'. In other words, the functionality that users were accustomed to would not be totally present in the new release. Only with a subsequent release of the software do the gains appear. So, the pain is in the first release, with the gain in the second. Where this occurs in a business change project (and most business change projects these days are underwritten by IT), the effect can be more dramatic. Business functionality can be less precise, thereby increasing the chances of misunderstood expectations.

Testing user perceptions may be thought to be difficult, but the benefit of at least making an attempt at testing must be better than doing nothing. Some physical approaches have proved particularly beneficial. Prototyping, for example, is a good aid for attempting to communicate the future vision. The 'model office' or the 'model working environment' expressed as physical layouts can help user communities and stakeholders visualise the change being created.

Even more explicit can be the 'usability laboratory', where users can be observed working through set business processes by designers, developers and trainers. Figure 22 (page 135) shows this in action. The model office is created behind a one-way mirror, through which cameras record the specific actions of users. The benefit is two-fold. The users get to see and play with the proposed environment. The developers see and fix the faults before any mass roll-out. (See Chapter 8, *Testing*, for more information on usability testing.)

Surveys and questionnaires can test the mood of a user

community for change, but unless expertly devised, can be subject to misinterpretation not only by the users but also by those analysing them. The direct interview approach is usually better, even if only for a sample of a large community. An experienced communications manager will select the best approach for the type of user audience and show how the currently familiar and comfortable can translate into the new ideal.

A colleague once told me that the best test of user acceptance was to offer to replace the new with the old a few weeks after implementation. If the offer was refused then the deliverable was acceptable. Reaching this point of 'mental ownership' is clearly a key outcome for the communications process.

Summary

The overall message is that expectation setting should not be left to chance. If it is, then the rumour mill will certainly undermine user expectations or even take them over completely. Because quality is a perception, its success relies on the human interpretation of the validity and applicability of what will be delivered. Expectation setting, therefore, requires particular effort to ensure that the human perceptions of all stakeholders are in line.

The project communication plan is a valuable contributor to user acceptance. It is, importantly, a living plan, and not a one-off document. Appointing a communications manager can ensure that specific and relevant plans are laid for the correct setting of expectations and, therefore, the achievement of acceptable deliverables.

4

Quality roles

Within a project or programme, all roles have a responsibility for ensuring that quality is built into everything they do. Certain project roles, however, have particular quality responsibilities, and some roles may be created that are concerned only with quality. These roles are examined below, starting with the project

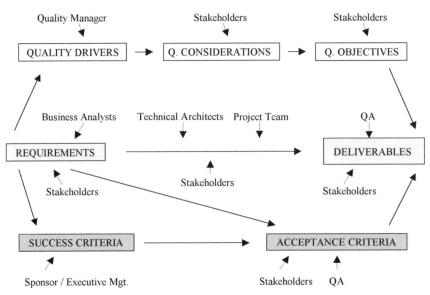

Figure 11: Typical roles applicable to key quality aspects

sponsor. Figure 11 is an expanded view of Figure 9, showing how typical roles interact with key quality aspects. It is assumed that the project manager and team would interact with all of the aspects. However, the translation of requirements into deliverables is specifically shown as the wider project team (ie, including any third parties).

The project sponsor

The business executive sponsoring a project or programme, known as the project sponsor or programme sponsor, bears a particular quality responsibility. This person needs to ensure that there is a commitment to quality within the project or programme that is commensurate with or exceeds that practised in the business. Where a client demands a different level of quality from that practised in the business, a sponsor needs to ensure that the business can meet that requirement.

A project or programme will rely on a commitment to a certain level of quality from the top of an organisation. A sponsor effectively acts as this interface, delivering that commitment and intervening when any difficulties arise. There are often particular pressures in the area of commitment. Pressures to curtail time, cost and quality are fairly common, such that a sponsor needs to be carefully balance business needs with those demanded by stakeholders.

A sponsor, however, should not be taken for granted. Awareness and communication need to be directed to a sponsor as much as to any other stakeholder. A sponsor cannot be expected to perform a quality role if expectations have not been set regarding the quality practices for a project. A sponsor may be a target when selling the benefits of employing a quality approach in a project, particularly if he has no previous direct experience of quality management. I mentioned in Chapter 3 the importance of selling the approach and ensuring that everyone was clear on what quality meant for a project.

In particular, a sponsor would be expected to protect vigorously the quality processes employed by a project, such as change control. Too often, businesses attempt to railroad the change control process, diluting its effect.

A sponsor often chairs a steering group, project or programme board. These are channels for a sponsor to stay in touch officially with a project, outside of any exceptional dialogue with a project or programme manager.

Typical quality tasks in the role of project or programme sponsor are, therefore, to:

- support the project or programme within the context of the business
- encourage the use of corporate quality practices
- support the commitment to quality within the project or programme

- be accountable for the feasibility of the project or programme within the business
- protect the validity and use of the change control process.

The project manager and team

A project manager is responsible for ensuring that quality management is properly implemented in a project and becomes an integral part of the overall project management processes. Certain responsibilities may be delegated to a professional quality manager, particularly where safety is critical, for example. Otherwise, a project manager might utilise in-house company quality resources and expertise.

The project manager should ensure that the project team understands the quality objectives and is committed to achieving quality in day-to-day work. The project manager should ensure that quality control activities are in place, where required, and that adequate measurements are selected for gauging the desired level of quality in deliverables and project management processes. Where applicable, earned value measurements may be utilised to assess performance of the team.

The project manager should also schedule quality assurance reviews at key milestone points, as required. These QA reviews will provide a formal checkpoint for assessing confidence in meeting the project objectives. Infrequently, the business or client may request a quality audit to be undertaken. The project manager should then ensure that auditors are selected external to the project and that any audit is conducted with minimal disruption to the project tasks and schedule.

Quality is the product of a state of mind, and so it is important that a project manager understands any human limitations within the team. He or she is effectively a champion of quality for the project, needing to foster the right attitude towards quality.

Typical quality tasks in the role of project manager and team are, therefore, to:

- ensure that quality management is properly implemented and practised within a project, and specifically to ensure that:
  - the team is aware of its responsibilities for quality
  - stakeholders are aware of their quality responsibilities
  - quality is adequately defined
  - a Quality Plan is produced and utilised
  - measurements are taken for conformance to standards and requirements
  - QA reviews are scheduled and take place
  - stakeholder expectations are set through an appropriate communication process
  - documentation standards are in place and followed
  - the change control process is followed.

The quality manager

If a quality manager is appointed to a project, he would accept the delegation of quality responsibilities from the project manager, leaving the project manager still *accountable* for quality. The quality manager's role would include most of the activities mentioned for the project manager, above.

The appointment of a quality manager, however, recognises that quality management is a professional activity, and that project managers are not, generally, highly skilled in this area. Using a quality manager ensures that the relevant quality processes are established and that the usually difficult task of quality definition is accomplished as quickly and as satisfactorily as possible.

Reporting to the quality manager would usually be quality assurers (unless these are planned to be utilised from outside of a project) and quality administrators. quality assurers would undertake QA reviews and advise teams on practical conformance. quality administrators would maintain the Quality Plan.

The quality team could operate from within a project office. Some might see this as a conflict of interest, but the only requirement to be impartial is really when external quality audits need to be undertaken. Some would also prefer to have the quality assurance function outside of the project. This is a matter of choice, though I believe in having as much quality self assessment within the project as possible, since this gives more accountability to the project team.

Typical quality tasks in the role of quality manager are, therefore, to:

- establish the quality management processes for a project, linking to existing business processes, where applicable
- establish the quality management function within a programme or project
- assist with the quality definition process
- act as quality consultant to a programme or project, guiding teams in the establishment and measurement of quality
- direct the work of quality assurers and quality administrators.

The quality assurer

Quality assurance may be carried out by one or more quality assurers in a project or programme. Whether a quality assurer is part of a project or programme team or is part of a business quality function will depend on the type of undertaking or company structure.

The role is not to build quality deliverables but to advise teams on how to ensure that the desired level of quality is being achieved. quality assurers look for evidence of compliance to standards or conformance to quality objectives. They may do this through scheduled QA Reviews, often at key milestone points or phase ends, or as required on an ad hoc basis.

The role is designed to be supportive. The Quality Plan will alert a quality assurer to the requisite quality criteria for a particular deliverable or set of deliverables. The Plan may point to detailed specifications held, not just within the project, but also with external suppliers. The QA role is particularly effective when dealing with external suppliers, since a quality assurer can provide a useful link between a supplier's development or manufacturing operation. This link can have less bias than a link between an in-house project developer and a supplier. A quality assurer can sometimes be a mediator in any disputes between supplier and project developer.

A quality assurer will be concerned with the complete life cycle of a deliverable, ensuring, from a quality perspective, that all components can be adequately integrated into the desired solution. It is likely that a quality assurer will compile, or have access to, checklists, in order to gauge compliance.

It is important that quality assurers are not involved at too late a stage in a project. A common mistake is to feel that because QA does not kick-in as a direct activity until after commencement of a project design phase it does not have any start-up activity. Certainly, quality assurers need to be involved in quality definition. Also, scheduled reviews need to be planned and QA processes need to be established.

Typical quality tasks in the role of quality assurer are, therefore, to:

- be involved in the quality definition process
- plan and undertake QA reviews and ad hoc audits
- establish links with suppliers and in-house functions producing deliverables or components

- review control measurements
- analyse and report on QA activities.

The quality administrator

One or more quality administrators may be required for a project or programme. A sizeable Quality Plan would need considerable administration, together with associated technical specifications. Scheduling of quality reviews, the compilation of reports and assistance to a quality manager or design manager would also be valid administrative activities.

In a recent, large, business programme, of which I was Programme Director, quality administrators also assisted the Communication Manager, and prepared and maintained the detailed stakeholder maps that I mentioned in Chapter 2. It is, therefore, useful for quality administrators to possess good communication skills and to ensure that they act in a supportive role to a project team.

Considerations for programmes

In a programme, the programme manager is accountable for the establishment of a quality environment – quality objectives, quality processes, etc. The programme should set standards for the operation and achievement of these, for its component projects. However, a sizeable programme might appoint a dedicated quality manager, who will be responsible for quality throughout the programme. Some programmes, using particular methodologies, would prefer to appoint a design manager, who would be part of the Programme Executive. A design manager (who may be part of a design authority) may also assume a quality role for a programme. (Refer to my book, *Managing Programmes of Business Change,* for a complete view of roles in a programme.)

All of these roles should ensure that standards, procedures and quality are maintained throughout the programme. Specifically, a design manager is guardian of the programme design, evaluating technical and business change requests against it to ensure that there is no dilution of benefits. In an IT or manufacturing programme, the design manager may well assume a more technical role. He or she might be an engineer, requiring a specific knowledge of safety critical operations or systems.

These roles may also act as consultants to the programme's projects, assisting projects to establish their own quality plans and dispensing advice concerning the management of quality. They will commission quality reviews and audits, as required, involving independent or third party reviewers as necessary. An initial piece of work will be to set quality standards, to which projects should comply, and to establish an overall programme Quality Plan.

Quality appears in many forms throughout a programme, and both the design manager and quality manager need to have a good understanding of its many guises. For example, Table 10 (overleaf) shows where quality may show itself in a business programme in which information technology plays a strong role.

The design manager will want to ensure that individual test plans are adequate for the level of quality desired. Testing will either be ongoing for each project or concentrated in discrete test phases. Prototyping and pilots are usually discrete test phases and may have a particular effect on the programme design. The Design may have to be adjusted to account for problems arising during these phases.

Besides addressing quality in general, the design manager and/or quality manager should monitor consistency of standards across projects in their scope and organisation, ensuring that change and issue control is adequately undertaken. They will need to ensure that dependencies between projects are mapped and that no duplication of work is undertaken.

Quality focus	Quality aspects
Business requirements	in terms of clearly stated and fully agreed requirements, programme briefs and project statements of work
Objectives	project objectives, sufficiently quantified and achievable
Benefits	realistic, understood and achievable
Deliverables	fit for purpose and conformant to requirements and standards
Marketing and communications	in terms of stakeholder identification and user expectations of what will be implemented
Contracts	sufficiently legal, including clear documents of understanding with suppliers and contractors
Training	focused on audience needs and capabilities
Documentation	in terms of project, training, support and user documentation, which is both readable and usable
Support	providing adequately staffed and trained support functions
Project management	providing for a properly estimated, planned and organised project through the use of reliable methodologies

Table 10: Typical quality areas in a business and IT programme

In a large programme they may retain a small staff, but many programmes will be able to utilise programme administrators in the programme office to perform administrative design management tasks.

The real opportunity for quality in a programme is through economies of scale. Where projects subscribe to a programme standard for quality, which is monitored by the programme office, desired levels of quality in projects may be achieved at reduced cost and resource. Table 11 shows an example of the dedicated quality roles in a large programme (300 personnel) that aimed to roll out business systems and processes to a nationwide user base. In this example, all roles, except the design authority operated from within the programme office. The large number of quality assurers was necessary to ensure geographic coverage.

Role	Activity
Quality manager	Responsible for programme quality; advise on conformance, expectation setting, etc.
Design authority (x2: manager plus assistant)	Maintain the programme design and assess the impact of technical change requests
Quality assurers (x4)	Assure quality at user sites during installation and set-up of systems and processes. Conduct quality reviews, as applicable
Quality Plan administrators (x2)	Administer the Quality Plan: maintain requirements, deliverables, quality objectives, stakeholder maps, assumptions, etc.

Table 11: Quality roles implemented in a large business programme

Summary

Everyone in a project needs to be involved in quality management. All project roles carry a responsibility for ensuring that quality is built into their activities. Particular project roles, such as a project sponsor, also have specific quality responsibilities. Specialist quality roles, such as quality assurers, complement the project team.

Programmes have a greater capacity for making economies of scale in quality management and can establish consistency in project management processes and practices. From a large programme to a small standalone project, quality is concerned with commitment. Those businesses that do not waver from practising rigorous change control and invest in good quality management practices, underwritten by a whole company commitment to quality, will have the most successful projects.

5

Planning for quality

The vital steps of quality definition (outlined in Chapter 2) are brought together in a Quality Plan, which becomes the day-to-day management plan for quality within a project or programme.

Although quality needs to be built in to every project management activity, the quality elements need to be recorded separately within a master Quality Plan. This allows a baseline for quality to be established and for adjusting the balance of quality required throughout a project. For example, the level of quality and its emphasis can be readily adjusted up or down if recorded centrally. The economy of scale to make these adjustments is not present if quality is viewed only in the context of a sub-project or work package. This is similar to recording separately the financial elements and the time schedule.

The Quality Plan sets the baseline for quality, but it would be wrong to assume that this baseline will never change. Approaches to quality need to be flexible, since the outcome can depend on, for example, design execution, experimentation, component integration and testing. However, it is important to ensure that quality is not exempt from the change control process.

Building a Quality Plan for deliverables

The Quality Plan is built up during the quality definition activity. It forms part of the overall project plan, and needs to be signed off like any other project planning document, and made subject to change control. What is it? What does it look like?

It is a sorry indictment that there are many projects that do not have a Quality Plan. This may be because, although many project management methodologies specify the need for one, they do not offer a template for the creation of one. It may also be that some projects believe that quality is somehow implicit within each of the work elements. However, my own experience shows that if quality cannot be identified specifically it cannot be managed. Too often, it is left to uncertainty whether quality makes any difference to the project outcome. This is, of course, not a desirable state of affairs, since quality can be identified, can be defined and can be managed to positive effect.

For me, the Quality Plan is a straightforward, uncomplicated document. It shows simply the project deliverables against stakeholders and requirements, how they will be controlled, tested, implemented and signed off as acceptable. It is, in fact, a very useful document – as useful as the cost plan, resource plan and time schedule, since these four documents form the core part of the management of a project.

Table 12 (overleaf) is a template that I like to use for a Quality Plan. It concentrates on deliverables, focusing on the quality required for a deliverable or product. Other quality elements I like to record in various project plans. For example, I would record how the project will be managed and the methodology and processes utilised in the master project plan. As another example, I would include the training of resources in quality management in the project resource plan.

Table 12 shows a Quality Plan in the format of a form. It can just as easily be produced as a standard text document, with respective headings. The form format makes for ease of use, since the document is designed as a working document and can be easily crafted as a computer-based form. Table 13 (overleaf) is a brief explanation of the fields in the form. Appendix B shows an example of a completed Quality Plan for one deliverable.

Completion of the Quality Plan needs some common sense. It may be feasible only to include the main deliverables of a project. A balance has to be reached, which is why the 'Importance ranking' field is important. I suggest a ranking of 1 to 10, to allow for a wide comparison of deliverables, but the number can be more or less. The ranking of deliverable importance should be carried out during the quality definition activity (see Chapter 2).

The 'Deliverable name' field is a shortened description of the deliverable, so that it may be easily referred to in reports and charts. The full description of the deliverable is allowed for in the 'Deliverable description' field.

'Deliverable owner' is an important field. It shows who has the day-to-day knowledge regarding the deliverable. Information about the deliverable can come from a number of sources, but in

QUALITY PLAN for *nn* Project

Deliverable Name	Id	Deliverable Owner	Importance Ranking	Current Status

Owning Sub-Project	Sub-Projects Affected	Stakeholders Affected

Deliverable Description

Components and their Origin

Production Cost	Maintenance Cost

Dependencies	Constraints

Associated Requirement(s)	Stakeholder Name(s)

Deliverable Producer	Deliverable Receiver

Integration and Usage Assumptions	Test Requirements

Acceptance & Handover Criteria	Quality Objective

Measurement Criteria

Test Sign-Off Requirements	Planned Delivery Date

Quality Review Schedule			
Quality Review	Date Scheduled	Date Held	Comments

Quality Plan Sign-Off		
Name	Position	Date Agreed

Table 12: Sample Quality Plan

QUALITY PLAN

Deliverable name and Id (shortened description)

Deliverable owner (who is responsible within the core project team for the deliverable)

Importance ranking (scale of 1 to 10 in terms of project criticality)

Current status (eg, requirement; specified; ordered; at design; in production; under test; delivered; installed)

Owning sub-project (the name of the sub-project or project function to which this deliverable belongs)

Sub-projects affected (the name of any sub-projects that are directly affected by the deliverable)

Stakeholders affected (the name of any stakeholders who are directly affected by the deliverable)

Deliverable description (full description)

Components and their origin (the components that make up the deliverable and where they are produced)

Production cost (optional)

Maintenance cost (optional)

Dependencies (anything the construction of the deliverable is dependent upon)

Constraints (known constraints that may affect the quality or production of the deliverable)

Associated requirement/s (the requirement(s) to which the deliverable is directly related)

Stakeholder name/s (the originating stakeholder(s), requesting the requirement)

Deliverable producer (may be the same as deliverable owner or responsible function or third party)

Deliverable receiver (the department or function in which the deliverable will be installed)

Integration and usage assumptions (how the deliverable will be integrated and used in operation)

Test requirements (test environment, type of testing and resources)

Acceptance & handover criteria (the stakeholder agreed criteria for acceptance of the deliverable into the using organisation)

Measurement criteria (how the deliverable will be measured for quality control)

Quality objective (the required level of quality or ISO Standard that must be met for the deliverable)

Test sign-off requirements (who needs to sign off the testing)

Planned delivery date (the date the deliverable is planned to be ready)

Quality review schedule (a note of any scheduled QA reviews or log of ad hoc reviews undertaken)

Table 13: Brief explanation of fields in the Quality Plan

order to avoid rumour and misunderstanding there should only be one person who owns the knowledge of the deliverable. This is particular appropriate when a deliverable is being created by a third party. The deliverable owner would be the person within the in-house project team responsible for the third party co-ordination concerning the deliverable.

'Current status' is a very useful field. It gives an instant lifespan position of the deliverable's progress. I suggest that a project defines a standard set of status fields that represent various positions of deliverable development.

Similar to deliverable owner is 'Owning sub-project'. This field shows to which sub-project the deliverable belongs for development purposes. It's an optional field, but one I find useful for reporting purposes.

You will notice that there is a strong link from the Quality Plan to the project communication plan. The fields 'Sub-projects affected' and 'Stakeholders affected' will indicate where expectation setting needs to be focused for each deliverable. 'Stakeholder name' applies to the person who has the requirement, and so would represent the principal stakeholder. This could be more than one person, of course, but it is important when there is a group to be able to specify one person who is accountable for the requirement. This name should be highlighted.

Stakeholders would also need to agree 'Acceptance criteria' and some would want to sign off their acceptance. Some projects like to involve their stakeholders in the sign-off of successful test stages also. This can be accommodated in the form. Specify also here the criteria for handover. How will handover be accomplished? (Refer to Chapter 9 for information on implementation and handover.)

'Components and their origin' is a field that allows a deliverable's components to be recorded. This is important because some components may be produced by different persons or third parties. A project needs to be able to construct a breakdown structure of deliverables and their components. Sometimes this may be obvious, but other times the cake may be cut in different ways, so to speak. For example, the project to write this book was broken down into deliverables that represent each chapter. Within each chapter were certain components such as figures and tables. The book itself, however, was the overall deliverable, so each chapter deliverable had to be integrated into the final whole. There are other ways in which the deliverables could have been specified. For example, all the figures could have been specified as one deliverable and all the tables another deliverable. My actual choice, though, reflected the way I wanted to produce the deliverables, and this is what a project must decide upon before constructing the Quality Plan.

'Production cost' and 'Maintenance cost' I have suggested as optional fields. For certain deliverables, it is useful to be able to weigh the level of quality against cost. If things become difficult in a project then these fields will help with the CTQ decision that will invariably need to be made.

The 'Dependencies' field is a good tracking field. Anything that a deliverable is known to be dependent upon may be recorded here. These dependencies can be tracked for completion. If any of the dependencies are assumptions, then these can be tracked for confirmation as decisions.

The 'Constraints' field represents known inhibitors to the successful construction of a deliverable. It may also refer to any risks identified in the project risk register. quality assurers will be particularly interested in this field, since constraints will affect the ability to produce the desired level of quality.

The 'Associated requirement(s)' field is the link to the origin of the deliverable. Since a deliverable may fulfil more than one requirement either in part or in whole, this field needs to state all the requirements it satisfies. I suggest that this field be used as a link to a separate, project requirements document, and that only the requirement ids be stated here.

Any quality standard that a deliverable needs to meet can be specified in the 'Quality objective' field, along with the quality objective itself. This is a standard output from the quality definition activity.

The 'Test requirements' field will need to state what testing must take place in order to prove conformance to the standard and quality objective. For third party developed components, a project manager needs to know what testing a third party has agreed to undertake and in what condition a deliverable will be handed over to the project for integration and completion. This field does not need to contain detailed test requirements, such as test scripts, but a summary of the test requirements and a pointer to other test-related documents.

'Acceptance criteria' are vital for deliverable testing. The 'Test requirements' field should, therefore, state the testing that will achieve acceptance. The acceptance criteria stated here are those that should have been defined during the quality definition activity.

'Measurement criteria' are discussed in Chapter 6. These relate to regular measurements that the project will take to ascertain that the desired level of quality is being attained. Any measurements that need to be taken during the construction of a deliverable need to conform to company or international standards, where applicable. Some deliverables require extensive quality controls during their design and construction, and need sophisticated measurements to be taken at various stages. Manufacturing projects, for example, may require the measurement of tolerances at fine levels and in many different situations.

Not all deliverables are easily measurable during deliverable design and production. Business processes, for example, may not lend themselves to 'hard' measurement. Usually, though, some form of regular, quantifiable checks can take place to ensure that the deliverable is being constructed to the quality objective. Formal quality assurance can then verify these checks.

The 'Quality objective' field is the heart of the Quality Plan. Everything else relates to it. It interprets the quality level for a deliverable, which is itself a product of a stakeholder requirement. The quality objective should not be ambiguous, but as clear and as quantified as possible. For deliverables with detailed technical specifications, the quality objective can refer to these rather than restate them.

The 'Test sign-off requirements' allows for a project to specify who needs to sign off that testing is complete and that a deliverable is in an acceptable condition for either integration or implementation.

The 'Planned delivery date' should reflect what is in the Project Schedule for a deliverable.

The 'Quality review schedule' is a working log of what quality reviews are scheduled and have been held. It can also include any quality audits called for the project.

The final task in preparing the Quality Plan is to obtain sign-off. Organisations have different requirements regarding sign-off, but I feel that, at the very least, the sponsor should sign off the Quality Plan.

Although deliverables are well catered for in the Quality Plan, some projects may need to record additional information – the associated design specifications, for example. The Quality Plan is flexible, but my advice is not to make it too unwieldy a document. Some items may be better recorded elsewhere, with the Quality Plan merely providing a link to these documents.

Apart from deliverables, the Quality Plan should include certain other items mentioned in Chapter 2. These are not deliverable-centric but items common to all deliverables. These include the quality definition map and other outputs from the quality definition workshop. Figure 12 in Chapter 6 is a useful diagram showing the links between the Quality Plan and other project documentation. Use this diagram to locate the obvious home for certain quality definition outputs. For example, the Map of Stakeholders is housed in the project communication plan, even though it may have been drawn up during a quality definition activity.

Knowledge management

I've included the topic of knowledge management (KM) under the heading *Planning for quality* because I believe it is something that needs to be considered right from the outset. This is because knowledge will be gained and needed right the way through the project lifespan, such that any investment in a knowledge repository will pay dividends.

Knowledge management is a quality function, not least because it can prevent re-work and foster re-use. Figure 12 shows just a few of the people needing to access and retrieve from a project repository.

Peter F. Drucker, in his paper 'The Coming of the New Organization'[1] , predicted that within 20 years from 1987 typical large businesses would operate with half the levels of management and one-third of the managers, citing information technology as the driver of an information-based company. Certainly, the opportunity for that exists now, but the problem that many companies have is in creating the disciplines to enable employees

1 Ref. *Harvard Business Review on Knowledge Management*

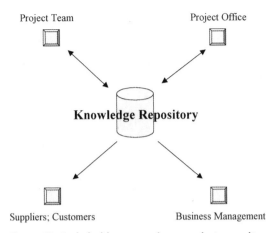

Project Team   Project Office

Knowledge Repository

Suppliers; Customers   Business Management

Figure 12: Stakeholders accessing a project repository

to deposit and retrieve the information as knowledge for re-use. From personal experience in more than one multinational company attempting to embrace the concept of knowledge management, I know that it is very difficult to motivate employees to make this happen. Access and retrieval have to be made simple and fast. For as long as the quickest and laziest solution is to re-invent the wheel, rather than look up past experiences, employees will not change their habits.

For repeatable undertakings such as projects, knowledge management has a vital role to play, and if companies can overcome cultural resistance, the time saved in just the launch of new projects can be phenomenal.

In a programme of change, it is often worthwhile to establish a responsibility for knowledge management within the programme. This might only be a link to an organisation's existing KM function, but the wealth of material being created in the programme might well justify additional heads. There are obvious links with document management, discussed in Chapter 6.

A project team has the opportunity to deposit its experiences as 'lessons learned' at project completion. The post-implementation review is the mechanism for deciding what went well and what didn't. However, both good and bad experiences need to be deposited. Organisations that are serious about project re-use will construct templates for the capture of key pieces of project information, such as various plans. Even with such prescription, there is a certain amount of post-project effort required to make this happen. Gantt charts, for example, can only be re-used with the tracking data stripped out. I like to see tasks on all project plans that provide for this post-project knowledge gathering. It is a worthwhile effort and should be planned for.

The knowledge needed for projects and programmes is typically in two forms: templates for setting up and controlling projects and information relating to specific previous experiences. Table 14 shows some examples in these two categories.

Project templates	Related project experiences
Gantt charts and time schedules	Estimates of effort for specific tasks
Generic work breakdown structures	Specific work breakdown structures
Resource plans	Skill sets
Risk register	Specific risks and treatments
Issue register	Specific issues and resolutions
Changes register	Specific changes and outcomes
Communication plan	Specific stakeholder categories and maps
Project plan master	Specific descriptions and paragraphs
Quality plan	Specific deliverables
Test plans	Specific tests
Project management processes	Paragraphs specific to project types
Acceptance criteria	Quantified acceptance criteria for specific deliverables types
Quality standards	Previous quality objectives and success rate
Measurement tools	Examples from specific deliverable types
Organisation breakdown	Organisation charts
Cost control plan	Previous financial records and success rates; earned value records
Documentation plan	Specific items of documentation of use to a project
Project office plan	Specific elements for rapid set-up of a PO
Post-implementation report	Specific previous reports

Table 14: Examples of knowledge re-use for projects

Of course, the biggest source of KM is the Internet. Each year, search engines become more sophisticated, enabling users to retrieve yet more precise project information. Companies that are able to utilise web-based project control should have easier access to templates for fast set-up. Project services automation (PSA) tools complement web-based control by linking to standard project accounting and performance monitoring. The general trend is for holistic, virtual, project workbenches, where everything is provided online, from know-how to project work creation and monitoring.

The great difficulty in implementing and maintaining a knowledge management system is encouraging the workforce to deposit and retrieve material. Companies and organisations have made various approaches towards this encouragement. Some have mandated the deposit of material, often against personal penalties. Some have offered incentives to those depositing material and those re-using previously deposited material. In my experience, many of these approaches have been failures. Expensive knowledge management systems often remain under-used in companies and organisations today. Where I have seen the most effective use of KM has been in companies where communities have evolved. Voluntary use of a KM system by a workforce that naturally understands the benefit is by far the best approach.

In one of my roles where I had responsibility for knowledge management in Europe, I noticed that only two areas regularly deposited and retrieved project management material in the KM system: Iberia and the Middle East. On a visit to the Spanish office, I very quickly discovered why. Here was a small and close-knit community of project managers which felt somewhat isolated by geography from the rest of the European region, so had established a practice of pooling their knowledge for the greater good. The situation in the Middle East was similar but with a difference. The spread of disparate individuals in different countries around the Middle East area forced them to seek a sense of belonging to a single body. Subscribing to the KM system helped relieve any sense of isolation.

Thus, a soft sell coupled with a natural desire to subscribe is what seems to work best for KM. We increasingly see websites encouraging participation. For example, a site advertising products might encourage visitors to append reviews of the products. This helps not only other enquiring visitors but the product company itself. The contribution, sharing and messaging environment that we see building up on the Internet can only assist the wider use of KM.

Summary

Planning for quality requires significant preparation at project start-up. Quality has often been the poor relation of CTQ, and a lack of good approaches has been a reasonable excuse to sidestep formal definition of quality for a project. Not any more. The techniques shown in this book prove that quality can be defined and planned, as much as cost or time, and that even though it is present in every project management element, it can be extracted for measurement, control and formal sign-off.

The Quality Plan is as important a project document as the time schedule, resource plan and cost plan. Projects that do not create one, risk delivering products that do not meet stakeholder expectations. Similarly, the lessons learned from previous projects are powerful knowledge, which can save considerable time during the planning and definition of quality.

Knowledge management can work well for a company or organisation if communities are allowed to evolve and are encouraged towards a common sense of purpose. Mandating users to practise KM often brings poor results.

6

Controlling quality

Using the Quality Plan to maintain control

As I said in Chapter 5, the Quality Plan is a living document. It should not be created and left on a shelf and referred to only occasionally. A project manager or quality manager can use the Quality Plan to:

- be confident that a baseline for quality has been defined, against which any change requests can be assessed
- ensure that all deliverables match one or more requirements

- ensure that stakeholders have been identified
- ensure that the project communication plan caters for targeted expectations setting
- ensure that acceptance criteria have been specified for all deliverables
- ensure that quality can be measured and tested
- control the effort of quality management commensurate with the quality objectives.

Effective use of the Quality Plan relies on an ability to link to various triggers. These triggers are usually expected dates or unexpected events. Some of these triggers will come from project plans and some from outside of the project. Figure 13 shows how certain fields in the Quality Plan link to other project documents and plans.

Expected dates are activities or milestones on various project time plans. If they occur on time then the Quality Plan is only affected if the achieved date refers to the production of something that is not of the right quality level.

Unexpected events could be dates missed on a plan. If a milestone is missed or an activity overruns, certain deliverables in the Quality Plan could be affected. Various types of delays are typical impacts to the Quality Plan and may manifest themselves as supplier problems, late documentation sign-offs, for example. Some unexpected events may appear as change requests. Their effect on the Quality Plan also needs to be gauged.

Totally unexpected events are those not normally shown on any plan. They may be the result of company acquisitions or market forces. If they affect the project, they may affect the Quality Plan.

I mentioned in Chapter 1 that I thought the Quality Plan could become a 'document of understanding' (DOU) between supplier and customer. This is certainly the case, even if there are no contractually binding acceptance criteria. The format of the Quality Plan lends itself to becoming a DOU. Setting out the quality criteria in such a baseline document enables all stakeholders to see what the project is working towards in quality terms.

Control of supplier quality is a particular requirement for many projects. Statements from suppliers such as: 'Just tell me what you want and I'll go away and do it and let you know when it's finished!' are clearly not acceptable to a project that is diligent in managing quality. A DOU helps to avoid this situation, by involving a supplier in regular dialogue.

Figure 13 shows that the status of a deliverable in the Quality Plan is linked to the development plan for that deliverable. Activities specifically related to quality need to be included in the project time plans (or schedule). Quality activities take time and effort as well as other project activities, so should not be excluded from project time plans. Quality reviews should also appear on project time plans as scheduled dates. Quality reviews also have a link to project risk registers, since the result of reviews can be the generation of new or changed risks. Any constraints shown on the Quality Plan are also linked to project risks.

Test requirements are also linked to project time plans, and also to any test plans. If test plans are changed, the Quality Plan needs to be checked for dependencies. The listing of deliverable dependencies in the Quality Plan will help in assessing any dependent changes that need to be made. The removal of a seemingly insignificant task or component on a plan could have a major effect on the quality of a deliverable as a whole. A good Quality Plan will show quality in the context of the whole project.

Stakeholder information is linked to the project communication plan. Changes to stakeholders in terms of responsibility, for example, need to be recorded. There is sometimes a tendency to treat a stakeholder change as a licence to

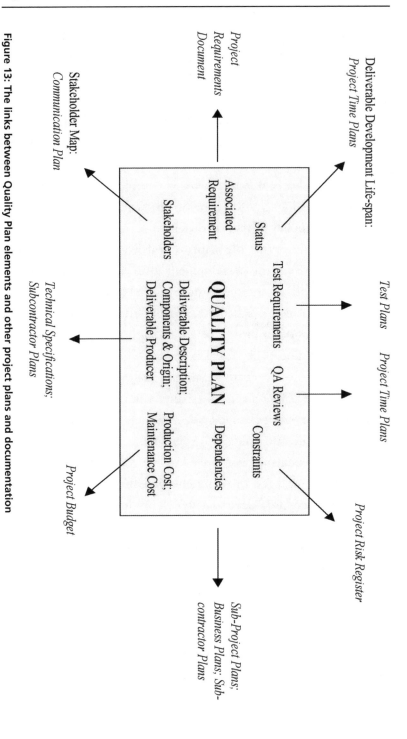

Figure 13: The links between Quality Plan elements and other project plans and documentation

make changes to deliverables. A new person coming into to an organisation may have different requirements. Any such changes, though, need to be passed through the change control process, if quality is to be maintained.

There is no reason why the Quality Plan should not be reviewed at regular project progress meetings. It is a good summary document, which tracks the progress of a deliverable through its status, tests, measurements, reviews and acceptance.

A particular problem with managing quality is scope creep. The scope of deliverables often increases incrementally and it is not always easy to pick up subtle changes.

Quality may well be affected, since the scope and specification of a deliverable may have changed unofficially during development from that agreed at project outset. Scope creep, though, may not be associated with any particular deliverable. A combination of small variances may occur across the project plan, making it difficult to pinpoint the problem. Regular reference to the Quality Plan and the undertaking of occasional specification reviews will help to highlight where there may be drift.

Controlling changes

Changes are inevitable with any type of project. It is inconceivable that a five-year IT project, for example, would ultimately deliver the technology it set out to. Unlike a programme, though, projects are not designed for significant change. A project is costed on its single, deterministic outcome, with perhaps a percentage being allowed for changes, but a project operates best with no changes. I say operates, because the works depends on mainly sequential tasks against a critical timescale. Interruptions to this sequence or timescale tend to be disruptive.

However, there are businesses that desire their client projects to regularly accept changes, because this is how they can improve their margins. They may sell a fixed price contract at an attractive rate in order to load it with changes that are expensive for their client. Scrupulous or not, this is how they make their profit. The project vehicle, though, is not best suited to this requirement, since the methodology is biased towards a stable work pattern. A programme, on the other hand, is specifically designed to evolve and change. Projects can be commissioned and decommissioned within a programme to accommodate and buffer the effects of change. If the wrong direction is being followed a programme can steer itself towards a new direction, without major disruption.

Change control is something many projects seem to just arrive at without overtly planning how changes will be managed. Yes, I know that many projects set up an electronic change control format, and but few take on board the real implications of change control with their clients at project outset. In other words, the technical process for change control may be established, but the important expectation setting with the client is often not done or given scant attention.

This expectation setting is vital at contract negotiation stage, especially if the contract is for a fixed price. Among other things, a client needs to understand the length of time that is realistic for his change request to be evaluated. This is because, in the midst of project execution, a client will inevitably demand a fast decision. However, the reality of project decision-making usually hinders the ability to give a fast answer. Why? Because there are likely to be many stakeholders who need to know about and give an opinion on the change.

Stakeholders will have different objectives for the change control process itself. A project team would generally prefer less change. A customer might prefer to be able to make as much change whenever he wants. A sales manager would want to keep his customer happy but might have a vested interest, via a sales target, in encouraging more chargeable change requests.

Change control is, therefore, a very human process. It relies on evaluations and opinions. Yet, it is fundamental to achieving good quality. It is not the purpose of this book to comment on the details of establishing a change control process or system, but to guide the reader to the particular areas of good and bad quality that exist within such a process.

One example of where a change control process can benefit is through the lessons learned from previous projects. This is particularly so where projects are repeatable undertakings, but even when they are not there is usually a finite amount of change types that can occur within an enterprise. Knowledge of how these were tackled and the results, in terms of resources, time, cost and quality, for example, is an important quality input. Since we have already learned that quality is about not re-inventing the wheel but drawing on past experiences to avoid rework, all projects intent on managing quality should have access to a knowledge database.

A fundamentally important consideration for change control is communication. I see many projects fall down through lack of attention to this. Because changes are classed as project exceptions, ie, exceptional events to the project baseline or normal course of work, stakeholders only become aware of their existence and progression through communication. It is my view that all project exceptions (eg, changes, risks and issues) should be discussed at regular, project progress meetings and their substance communicated to interested parties.

Automated change control systems often have the ability to provide some automatic communication. They might, for example, be able to advise all interest parties by email when a change request has been received. They may also show the current status of a change, visible to anyone who may access the system.

However, even here, there is a human interaction required, which, if lacking, can make a mockery of the benefits of the automation.

The most basic form of communication that is required, however, is training for all stakeholders in the change control process. This, as I mentioned in the section *Reading the stakeholder audience* in the *Setting expectations* chapter of this book, is not about sending out a lengthy, change control process document for people to read and adhere to. It is about ensuring that each step of the process is understood, particularly in terms of its importance within the process. Customers and suppliers, especially, need to understand what is involved.

So, what are the quality considerations for change control?

- Stakeholder buy-in and commitment to the change control process
- An appreciation by stakeholders of the length of time each stage of the change control process is reasonably expected to take
- Adequate communication of changes to stakeholders
- Stable baselines, particularly project scope
- Access to knowledge of previous change situations
- Full understanding of contractual requirements.

Configuration management

The most important input to the change control process is the project baseline. This is the yardstick against which all changes should be evaluated. The baseline would, of course, change upon the implementation of a project change, so configuration management becomes an important associated process. So much so, that some projects manage changes within the configuration management process. Software for change control may also include configuration management.

Configuration management is the control of the blueprint of

project deliverables, from their design through to construction and eventual implementation. These are also known as products in some project management methodologies. The project plan keeps track of the work development, which means that there are effectively two baseline vehicles for a project, against which changes need to be evaluated: the project scope and the deliverable or product scope.

Configuration management records and tracks the physical components of deliverables, the baselines for a project (in terms of designs, standards, plans and project procedures), together with a history of their versions and releases into a user environment. Each configurable component (deliverables, designs, standards, plans, procedures, etc.) can be broken down to its lowest manageable component. These are known as configuration items (CI). These days, there are several sophisticated software packages that cater for configuration management, so no one needs to keep track of configurations on scraps of paper.

So, what are the quality considerations for configuration management?

- Due diligence in the accurate recording of baselines and components
- Due diligence in the release of versions to a user environment
- Support for the quality review and audit process
- Accurate and timely communication of configuration items to stakeholders
- Protection of secure components and documentation
- Ability to assess project changes against baseline configurations.

A good configuration management process relies on accurate and timely input. In a project development phase, versions may quickly be superseded, particularly with respect to documentation. The discipline of reporting this information to the configuration controller needs to be enforced by the project manager. Here there is some benefit in having an automated reporting system for configuration management.

Version control

Version control is a subset of configuration management, but has such significance in terms of quality, that it deserves special discussion. So many projects have foundered in user acceptance terms on poor version control, yet it is not a difficult process to get right.

When companies were making preparations for the Year 2000 computing crisis, version control became a vital issue. It was very evident whether companies had practised good version control if details of installed components that might fail after December 31st 1999 could be verified. Countless situations came to light in both manufacturing and computing where adequate records of versions were lacking.

Version control can be a particular nightmare when developing software. Many versions of a piece of code can be created during a single day, making it relatively easy for new versions to be overwritten by older versions. I remember a particularly expensive error when the wrong version of software was rolled out to more than 800 users in retail outlets. The person with the right disc had gone on holiday.

In mechanical and electrical engineering, there are often versions within versions, such that control of nested components needs to be carefully managed. Superficially, something might seem to be the right version, but the components inside prove otherwise.

It is often difficult to discern what version a component is, let alone whether it is the latest version. Documentation is notorious for this. Unfortunately, certain automated aids in word processing software have been less than satisfactory in this respect. Is the date on a piece of documentation the printed date, the revised date, the file saved date or the original date? It is often not possible to say.

Certainly, a good configuration management system should be able to say; but it would be useful in an environment of changing components to be able to inscribe the version number on the component itself.

Quality considerations for project version control are, therefore:

- Ensure that there is a good baseline for all deliverables and components
- Track versions and releases in a configuration management system
- Ensure that component dependencies are understood and logged
- Where possible, inscribe the version number on a component
- Ensure that the status of a version is rigorously logged (ie, is it live, in test, or superseded by a later version?).

Don't forget, project documentation is itself a component.

Document management

British Standard 5750 has a lot to say about document management, and rightly so. The standard effectively states that any single sheet of paper must be identifiable to a host document. This is particularly important in a project situation, when there are many sheets of paper in evidence at any one time. I have, on many occasions, picked up odd sheets of paper lying around (mostly around shared printers), which are difficult to identify in terms of owner or host document. Many of these have been highly sensitive documents. Security is just one quality aspect that affects documentation; ownership, version and identity are others.

A problem for most projects is that documentation comes in various guises. It can be a written procedure, an email, electronic help text, a spreadsheet, a graphical presentation, a marketing brochure, just to name a few. All need to be protected, however, whether for security, copyright or quality.

In projects that I manage, I always advocate the use of a documentation standard. If the host organisation does not have an existing standard then I compile one. This includes a security classification, and is designed to ensure that each piece of documentation is identifiable. The principle is simple. Each piece of documentation should state:

- a security classification
- a page number
- a version number and date
- a title of the document and any reference
- originator's (or owner's) name or initials
- copyright notice (where applicable).

A typical security classification may comprise:

- Unclassified
- Internal use only
- Company (or client) confidential
- Restricted.

Most companies and organisations will have their own interpretations of what these mean. It is important, however, to state whether a document is unclassified, even though it may be assumed as a default. By having a security classification and a policy describing it, anyone finding a document knows what to do with it. For example, confidential documents should not be left lying around on desks, even during a working day. Documents left unclaimed around a printer at the end of a working day may be disposed of accordingly.

The document page number is also important. It shows where a single sheet fits in relation to a complete document. Ideally, the ascription should be 'Page n of n', in order to show how many pages comprise the complete document.

Version number and date help decide the currency of a document. In a project, there are often numerous versions of the same document in circulation at any one time. It is important to know which version is which, particularly when in discussion.

Document titles and any library or catalogue references are also important. A single sheet may belong to a chapter or section within a master document. It is helpful to be able to discern where a sheet belongs.

The originator or owner of a document should also be stated. This is usually abbreviated for practical reasons, but should be identifiable nonetheless. The full details of originator and owner should appear at the beginning of a document, after the title page.

Finally, copyright is an important statement to make, in order to safeguard intellectual property. A copyright notice (where applicable) should appear on every page.

Appendix C is a draft of a generic documentation standard, which you may want to tailor for your projects, if you do not have any existing company standard. It is not exhaustive, but demonstrates a minimum standard for good documentation control. Most companies set up documentation templates, for use in various types of software (word processing, spreadsheets, graphics, email, etc.), so that it is easy for their employees to conform to the documentation standard.

Of course, document management is not just about ensuring traceability and the correct classifications for security and copyright, it is also about being able to classify, file and retrieve the myriad information circulating around a typical project.

Knowledge management, as I mentioned in Chapter 5, is a real benefit not only for an existing project but also for future projects. At any time during a working day, project personnel will need to be able to access information. How quickly they are able to do this depends on the knowledge system installed. If information from past experiences has been classified for easy retrieval and re-use then its value will be priceless.

Some projects feel the need to appoint a document manager, as they know they will be relying on having an efficient means of cataloguing and retrieving project material. There will, of course, be a requirement for project personnel to exercise due diligence when compiling and filing project material. A process and system are only as good as those using it. There will be occasions when documentation will need to be retrieved quickly, such as for audits and reviews.

Measuring project quality

The measurement of project quality directly relates to its definition. If you cannot define it, it cannot be measured or even built. However, some things are easier to measure than others. The initial question project managers need to answer in terms of measurement is: what needs to be measured?

If a project needs to conform to quantifiable standards, then appropriate measurements need to be set up. For tangible components and deliverables, the taking of measurements can be quite sophisticated. Measures of stress in construction materials and measures of luminosity in paint finishes, for example, can be carried out using special equipment. For less tangible things, measurements may need to be quite creative. A business process, for example, may be measured in terms of throughput per day.

Efficiency and performance are quality drivers and can be measured accordingly.

The Quality Plan needs to state the measurement requirements: what measurements are appropriate, who is going to undertake the measurements, where and when. Measurements may need to be taken at specific times or over a particular period. Each organisation should know what is required in measurement terms for business, standard conformance, regulatory or certification purposes.

From a quality point of view, measurements provide soundings of the state of a component or complete deliverable. These soundings can be used to control quality by making adjustments, as necessary. A software programmer, for example, might want to measure the efficiency of a block of code, by checking how many system resources are used in its execution. This can bring a sort of local confidence, but he cannot test for overall performance, however, since other criteria are needed to be brought into play. Overall confidence can only be gained by applying all the constraints of a normal operation, usually in a usability test or pilot.

Measurements, therefore, have a particular use in the control of quality during production, and provide valuable input to the quality assurance function. This latter function is designed to take a wider view when reviewing a deliverable, interpreting the level of quality achieved against the quality objectives and stakeholder requirements.

Measurements can continue to be taken during user testing and a pilot phase. In fact, some measurements need to be transferred to the business after handover, since quality may need to be continually monitored after the project has been completed: production of foodstuffs, for example. Figure 14 (overleaf) shows this graphically.

Some measurements are taken as samples. For example, the relative frequency of a situation occurring may be assessed. A business case may only include estimates. For example: 'We estimate the number of calls to the support desk will be *nn* out of

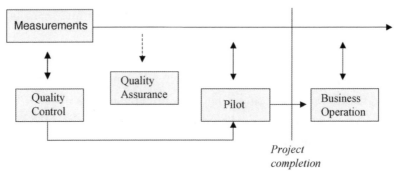

Figure 14: Typical measurement pathway from quality control into the business operation

a total of *nn* for this product'. During usability testing these estimates may be refined through the taking of specific measurements.

Under project conditions, the opportunities for measurement are confined to the project lifespan, but in a programme the opportunities may extend beyond a single project lifespan but still remain under control of the programme. This means that measurements such as those to test ongoing customer satisfaction do not have to be confined only to the steady-state business operation. In a programme, a project may complete and the satisfaction of a customer may be assessed for a following period. If satisfaction is rated as poor then further work may be commissioned by the programme to improve it.

The measurement of customer satisfaction is undertaken by many companies as a test of quality in service or product. Some may utilise a questionnaire format to calculate a rating either once after product or service delivery or as an ongoing periodic measurement. A programme quality manager or business change manager are roles well placed to conduct quality measurements within a business or user community.

Quality measurements, though, do not have to be against things that have been developed or are in the progress of development.

Measurements of quality may be made right from the start of a project or programme. Techniques for rating the applicability of stakeholder requirements to technical or business functions, for example, are particularly useful aids to the quality definition process.

QFD House of Quality is one such technique. QFD or 'quality function deployment' helps to translate stakeholder requirements into product development requirements, and is simply constructed (ideally in a group session). QFD consists of four phases: product planning, taking stakeholder requirements; parts deployment, taking design requirements; process planning, selecting a production process to be used; production planning, taking the production requirements. The House of Quality is a planning chart that represents the output of the first phase of QFD: product planning. Figure 15 shows an example of the format. For the purposes of this

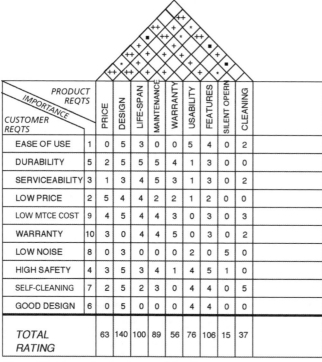

PRODUCT REQTS	IMPORTANCE	PRICE	DESIGN	LIFE-SPAN	MAINTENANCE	WARRANTY	USABILITY	FEATURES	SILENT OPERN	CLEANING	
EASE OF USE	1	0	5	3	0	0	5	4	0	2	
DURABILITY	5	2	5	5	5	4	1	3	0	0	
SERVICEABILITY	3	1	3	4	5	3	1	3	0	2	
LOW PRICE	2	5	4	4	2	2	1	2	0	0	
LOW MTCE COST	9	4	5	4	4	3	0	3	0	3	
WARRANTY	10	3	0	4	4	5	0	3	0	2	
LOW NOISE	8	0	3	0	0	0	2	0	5	0	
HIGH SAFETY	4	3	5	3	4	1	4	5	1	0	
SELF-CLEANING	7	2	5	2	3	0	4	4	0	5	
GOOD DESIGN	6	0	5	0	0	0	4	4	0	0	
TOTAL RATING		63	140	100	89	56	76	106	15	37	

Relationship

++	Strong	5
+	Good	4
Δ	Medium	3
∗	Weak	2
■	Poor	1
O	None	0

Figure 15: Example of a House of Quality

book, I will concentrate on the House of Quality. There are several books dealing with the QFD process for those readers wishing to understand how the total process may be utilised.

Looking at Figure 15 you can see that the House of Quality is constructed in several sections. These sections can be used as appropriate to your project. To the left is a summary of the customer (or principle stakeholder) requirements. Along the top is a summary of the product features. At the centre is the relationship matrix, which correlates the customer requirements with the product features. Various ratings can be used for this, but the example shows a rating of 0 to 5 (where 5 is the strongest match of requirements to features, 1 is the poorest match and 0 means there is no match). This rating can be made by members of a project team and averaged to a single score. The customer requirements are ranked in order of importance. The area to the right of the relationship matrix may be used for additional rating purposes. It is sometimes used for evaluating a product against its competitors. The House of Quality is not complete without a roof, which shows the cross-relationship of product features. Finally, the ratings in the relationship matrix are multiplied by the customer requirements importance rating and added to give a total rating. In the example, design (with a score of 140) is rated as the product feature that most matches the overall customer requirements.

The House of Quality is not a scientific measurement, but it does give a good feel for stakeholder perception. Compiling the chart is best done in a group session. This generates buy-in and ensures that as representative a section of stakeholders is made as far as possible.

Other measurements that can be made from the start of a project are decision trees. Figure 8 in Chapter 2 and Figure 19 in Chapter 8 are examples. The comparison of one or more options based on the probability of the options occurring and their relative cost is a useful quality assessment. Again, team input is encouraged here.

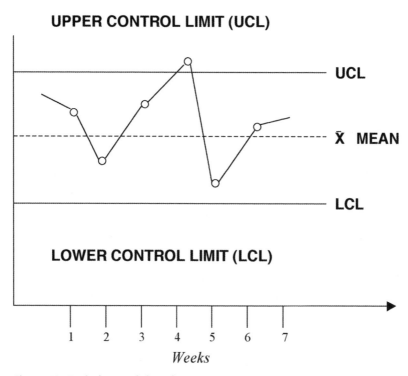

Figure 16: Typical control chart format

Some projects may benefit from using *statistical process control* (SPC), which is a measurement of process stability. Where processes can be modelled and observed, control charts can be constructed to measure whether a process is in or out of control. The measurement depends on identifying a customer's perception of performance standards and tolerances. These are used as a baseline from which regular monitoring is undertaken. Figure 16 shows a typical control chart format, with a process out of control at Week 4. Their construction requires the calculation of upper and lower control limits – a not insignificant statistical exercise.

There are many other types of chart that can be constructed to show measurements of quality[1]. A good quality manager will

1 Refer to publications such as *The Memory Jogger* (see Bibliography).

know what forms of measurement and charting are appropriate for a project.

Before leaving the subject of measuring quality it is important not to forget the performance and efficiency of the project itself. How a project performs is a statement of quality, so it is appropriate to instigate some form of project measurement. Certain types of project have specific measurements of project performance, such as the efficiency of lines of code in software development projects, for example. A good generic performance measurement, though, is *Earned Value*.

Earned value (EV) is a technique that shows how much has been 'earned' by the completion of project tasks against a baseline budget and schedule. It shows the actual cost of work performed against the budget and variances in the cost and schedule. Some project scheduling tools have the ability to calculate this from data entered into the software application, but in order to calculate Earned Value a project plan needs to be properly tracked.

In a traditional approach to managing project expenditures against costs only three variables are available: the planned cost value, the actual cost value, and the budget. The addition of a fourth value (the earned value), which is based on the percentage of work completed at any given time, helps to reveal the true cost of the project. Figure 17 shows this graphically. For example, a project that has a budget of £10,000 and has actual costs of £2,000 against a planned position of £3,000 at the time of review would seem to be in reasonable shape. However, calculation of the earned value reveals an EV figure of £1,000. £3,000 less £1,000 is £2,000, which means the project is £2,000 behind where it is planned to be. The project is also overrunning its costs by £1,000, since the EV of £1,000 less the actual costs of £2,000 is minus £1,000. Put another way, of the £10,000 budget, only £1,000 has been achieved at a cost of £2,000.

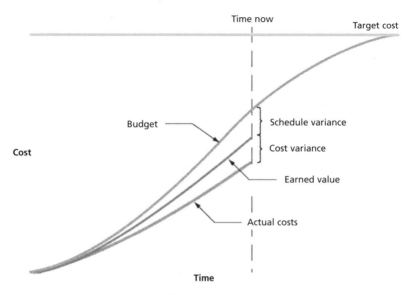

Figure 17: Graphical representation of earned value against budget and actual costs

Governance

The formal control of a project or programme is usually executed through governance.

The governance of a project or programme needs to be set into the context of its business. Thus, there should be a corporate governance structure into which a project or programme will need to fit. Each company or organisation is likely to have its own ground rules for the governance of projects. However, there are some generic standards that can be applied to all projects. In general, steering groups or boards will look for projects to be operating efficiently and effectively, and they will require information to enable them to reach conclusions and to make decisions regarding their direction.

A project manager or programme manager will undertake regular progress reviews (usually weekly or fortnightly) and probably expect a consistent form of reporting from project personnel. This may be packaged for use in reporting to senior stakeholders, who, depending on the methodology chosen, will hold steering group meetings or formal project or programme boards, usually on a monthly basis. There is, therefore, a reporting cycle of reviews and meetings that make up the governance process.

The governance process for a project or programme needs to be established at the outset. If a list of stakeholders has been compiled, then it is relatively easy to compile their reporting needs and construct a governance timetable covering a monthly or quarterly period. The needs of each stakeholder will be different, of course. A project manager will need sufficient detail to be able to manage the project on a day-to-day basis. A project board, however, needs only sufficient detail to ensure that the project is being efficiently managed and on the right track.

If a programme or project is utilising a PSA tool, different levels of stakeholders should be able to pull off reports in a format commensurate with their needs. The dashboard approach is frequently utilised and is designed to give a quick view of key components such as risk and milestones in an integrated format. Frequently, traffic light indicators (red, amber, green) or high, medium and low gradations are used to show whether something is under control or out of control. Figure 18 shows some dashboard components. These may be performance indicators (such as earned value), efficiency indicators (such as resources utilisation) and indicators of effectiveness (such as milestones completed). PSA tools can compose these automatically. Otherwise, a project office would have to compile the data and charts manually.

It is easy to over-govern and impose a straitjacket on a project manager. The boundaries and tolerances for control need to be established at outset. A project manager must have room to exercise his responsibility. I once found myself in a ludicrous

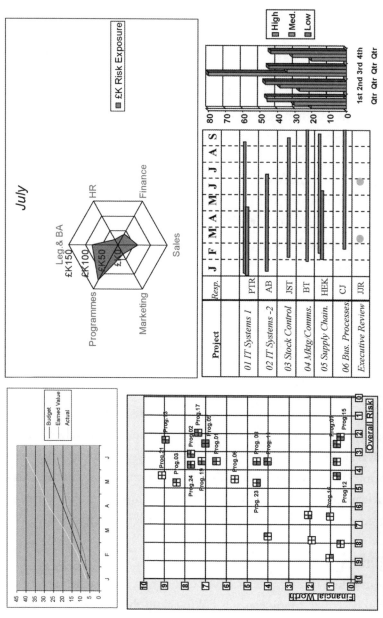

Figure 18: Key indicators can be represented in a dashboard approach

situation where I was required to attend 40 programme boards each month. Yes, the programme was large and very high value, but size should not be an excuse for over-governance!

Some questions to bear in mind when exercising governance are:

- Is the prescribed programme or project methodology being followed?
  - Have exceptions or short-cuts been made?
  - Are any management roles missing?
- Is the project or programme running to time, cost and quality?
  - Are reliable statistics being compiled and made available to assess these?
- Is the performance at maximum possible efficiency?
  - Is value being earned?
- Is the business placing undue constraints on the project or programme?
- Are required standards being met?
- What aspects are preventing the project or programme from meeting its objectives? (eg, funding, resources, skills, time)
- Is there faith in the outcome?
  - In what state is morale?

This last question is important, since it is easy to forget the human aspects of a project or programme in the governance process. Governance is not just about checking physical progress; it is also about establishing whether the operational climate and environment are right. A happy team is one that will strive to succeed. Therefore, indicators of morale are just as important.

Summary

Controlling quality is heavily dependent upon the achievement of valid baselines. Many projects fail to spend the important up-front time in establishing these. The Quality Plan is a good baseline document, which can link to all the other quality-related documents. The development of trigger points for re-assessing quality will help to signal when specific action is needed. Change control and configuration management are key processes for producing such triggers.

Because quality is a perception there can be huge variances in the results of measurements taken. However, these variances can deliver useful messages by comparison, so are well worth measuring. A single measurement means very little, but in comparison to many others, especially over time, it can mean a great deal.

The overall level of quality in a project or programme is formally controlled through governance. Good governance is not bureaucracy but a means of ensuring that there are no surprises and that a project or programme is operating efficiently and effectively to the required standards.

7

Quality assurance

While individuals in a project have day-to-day responsibility for ensuring quality is built in to whatever they are working on, there is usually little opportunity for them to step back from the detail and take stock of a complete package of work. The ability to take this wider view and to ensure that individual aspects of quality are applied in the context of the whole project is part of the function known as quality assurance (or QA, as it is commonly known). QA applies this big picture of quality to give the confidence that deliverables are being designed and developed according to the requirements and the appropriate standards. It is very much a gradual build-up of checks and balances that take place over a project's lifespan – each one giving increasing confidence (or not) that the outcome will have the right level of quality.

There is often confusion between quality assurance and quality control (QC). QC is the ongoing control and measurement of quality, whereas QA is the check that everything is going to plan (the Quality Plan in this case). QA, therefore, tends to manifest itself mainly as scheduled reviews or audits.

If a project has appointed a quality manager, then that person will be responsible for ensuring that QA takes place. Some project managers will prefer to utilise a company quality function to perform QA activities for their projects. This may give a more impartial opinion.

In a project, QA is limited to the development and implementation of deliverables, plus the project management system. In a programme, QA can extend beyond the implementation of a single project, enabling the programme to take corrective actions if quality is not being upheld in the user environment.

The Quality Plan is the main input to the QA process, along with relevant detailed specifications and plans. QC is also a prime input to the QA process, since the ongoing control and measurement of quality will show whether the quality objectives are being met.

QA takes various forms, and these are mainly variations of quality checking, from inspections and walkthroughs to sampling, reviews and audits.

Inspections and walkthroughs

The easiest way to check for quality is through inspection. Inspection can be used for physical components and deliverables as well as business procedures. As long as the limitations are understood, inspection can be a useful first feel of quality, and, in many cases, the comfort factor derived from an inspection can be carried forward to reality. The production of metal castings for assembling a new mobile phone product, for example, can be visually inspected and their operation by end-users in the final product can be envisioned. However, inspection is no ultimate guarantee, since true quality can only be ascertained within a total situation. Only user testing can provide the additional comfort factor that the castings will be fit for purpose. Components may be inspected for defects, but the operation of the component in context is what ultimately counts. Also, inspection is often not feasible for large quantities of components. In this respect, projects usually prefer to take a representative sample.

Sampling is often used as a gauge of quality, and we all know from political opinion polls how unreliable this approach can be. Even in usability testing, there is no guarantee that the user group conducting the tests is exactly representative of the total. It does seem to instil confidence with project teams, though, and has merits, as long as the limitations are understood.

Inspection and sampling may be undertaken during quality control and, more formally, within the quality assurance process. Under QC, there may well be standard checklists employed for the inspection of components. Under QA, these checklists may be utilised for a more formal, and often independent, review.

Inspection is just one means of checking quality levels. Another is the *walkthrough*. This is a step-by-step appraisal of a system or process for the benefit of selected stakeholders. It is in some ways a form of envisioning[1], since the person conducting the walkthrough interprets for stakeholders' benefit the written description of a process. It can be done at any time, and successive

1 Refer to Chapter 8.

walkthroughs will help to build greater confidence in the ultimate product.

Walkthroughs are popular in IT, where they are undertaken at several levels. A design team, for example, may be given a walkthrough of design concepts or end-users may be given a walkthrough of part of a system. As with inspections, walkthroughs ultimately need to be taken in context. They can be like component testing – always outlooking the integration tests.

Quality reviews

The prime opportunity for conducting quality assurance in a project is through a series of scheduled QA reviews. These should be planned during the quality definition process. They can be scheduled according to provisions in a contract or at relevant milestones or phase ends. Funding for the reviews, which could be expensive if external resources are brought in to carry out the reviews, should be earmarked at project outset. There should always be contingency for ad hoc reviews that may need to be called, particularly if indications suggest there may be quality problems. Control charts, for example, may indicate *special causes* (abnormal causes of variation in a process), which could trigger an ad hoc review. Either way, the quality manager and quality team (if appointed) would advise on appropriate review schedules and formats.

The Quality Plan should drive the review process. The Quality Plan refers to the measurement criteria and test criteria for deliverables, plus the quality objectives and acceptance criteria, all of which are necessary information for a QA review. The Plan also states the sign-off required for QA reviews.

If problems with the level of quality are discovered during a QA review, changes may need to be requested through the change control process. In practice, there should be no real surprises during a QA review, if there have been close dialogue, communication and reporting of deliverable progress. If there are surprises, it could be said that the project management system has not been operating at a quality level. Regrettably, it is often poor communication that lets projects down in this respect.

Some contracts hold suppliers accountable for passing QA reviews before proceeding to the next stage of a development. This makes it even more important to ensure that adequate preparation for reviews is made.

It is not practical in this book to detail the processes for QA reviews. Companies and organisations will usually have their own processes, based on experience. Some considerations can be mentioned, however. Firstly, it is important to differentiate whether the review is targeting specific deliverables or aspects of the project management system. The format of the review will be different in each case. The former will focus mainly on technical aspects while the latter will focus mainly on human aspects.

Some generic considerations for deliverables are:

- Do they conform to standards, where required?
- Do they conform to requirements?
- Are there clear and detailed specifications?
- Is there good, supporting documentation?
- What tests have been carried out to date?
- What components have been integrated?
- What quality objectives do they meet now, and are proposed to meet later?
- Is development on plan?
- Are there any outstanding issues, risks or changes?
- What logs are being maintained?
- What measurements have been undertaken or are in the process of being undertaken?

Some generic considerations for the project management system are:

- Is everyone aware of the current status of the project within its lifespan?
- Have all plans and procedures been drawn up according to the requirements of the project management methodology? Are there any exceptions?
- Is the risk register current and are risks being managed?
- Is an issue log being maintained? Are issues being resolved?
- Is the change control process being rigorously applied?
- Is the quality plan current and is quality being managed?
- Is the communication plan being managed?
- Are stakeholder expectations being managed?
- Are progress meetings being held and are they effective?
- Are milestones being achieved?
- Is value being earned on the project schedule?
- Is everyone on the project team aware of their roles and responsibilities? Do they have job descriptions and performance objectives?
- Is there a project office and is it supportive?
- Is there a skills map and resource plan for project personnel?
- Is training and education planned and taking place for project personnel?

It is important to remember that QA reviews are snapshots in time. Some things may not be fully in place when a review is held. Also, the reviews need to be supportive. If a review is perceived to be like a formal audit, there will be insufficient co-operation between the reviewer and the person being reviewed. The best quality approach for a QA review is one of support. The reviewer will often have greater experience than the person being reviewed and this experience should be shared. Reviews, in my experience, can be excellent training grounds for busy project personnel.

Summary

Quality assurance is designed to bring confidence to the project manager, the team and stakeholders. It should be treated as a positive experience, where the whole project benefits, and, of course, eventually the end-user organisation.

The Quality Plan should drive the QA approach, bringing in all the necessary components from its linked plans and processes. The ultimate aim is success. Faith in the outcome is an important cultural requirement that can be underwritten by good QA practice.

8

Testing

Testing is an activity that is fundamental to proving quality. It seeks to demonstrate whether a deliverable or deliverable component works to the desired specifications.

It is not just about this, though. It is also about whether expectations have been met. The latter is not often appreciated by those involved in testing, and I have many experiences of this being a cause for considerable argument. Some testers will openly state that their role is not to test for something working as expected. This is a big mistake, and is symptomatic of a poor mindset towards quality. If expectations have been managed well during the execution of a project then there should not be any mismatch of expectations. However, some projects tend to have more indefinite deliverables than others – software development projects, for example. In this case, prototyping is an added safeguard to the risk of expectations mismatches during final testing.

Companies and organisations take various approaches to testing and these approaches will vary depending on the project. Engineering projects, for example, may require extensive and detailed testing of components, with the setting up of a sophisticated test bed. IT roll-out projects may require a pilot installation to iron out any problems prior to mass roll-out. Aeronautical projects may require the building of a prototype aircraft in order to demonstrate proof of concept. Software development projects may require a period of parallel running before replacing one system with another. Outsourcing projects might benefit from the construction of a model office environment to test a new work-place.

Testing, therefore, comes in various guises. It does not have to be a discrete phase in a project, but can be ongoing right from project outset. The purpose of this chapter is not to provide guidance on which testing to use, but to explore it from a quality perspective. In doing this, various types of testing will be discussed, each of which will aid the achievement of a particular aspect of quality. Figure 19 shows a possible testing pathway from requirements to deliverable implementation. Again, the exact approach taken to testing will vary according to company and project.

It shows that the components of a deliverable may be tested individually and subjected to individual stress testing. The integration of components into a whole may then be tested, with the whole also being subjected to stress testing. Volume testing can apply a different form of stress, prior to user testing. This latter

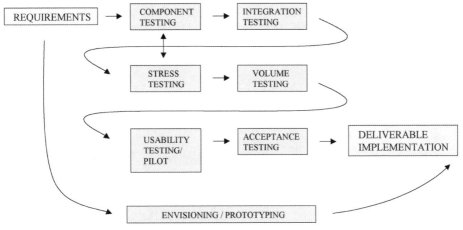

Figure 19: Possible testing approach

could take the form of usability testing or pilot (rarely are both required), prior to final acceptance testing and implementation.

Above all, testing will be subject to the appetite of a company or organisation for testing. It is often a cultural thing. Risk takers may be less inclined to undertake testing than those who are risk averse. It is also representative of confidence – confidence in the product and its ability to do the job.

Envisioning

Because quality is a perception and, therefore, subject to human interpretation, the proof that a deliverable is working is not enough. It has to work to the satisfaction of all stakeholders. The example of the Bremen Space Centre described in Chapter 3 shows the effect of not having total agreement. This means that testing must absolutely consider stakeholder expectations. This is quite a departure from traditional views of testing, and requires a new form. This new form is widely known as *envisioning*. It has similarities with the concept of prototyping, in that stakeholders are shown a vision of what the future could look like. This could be for a project or programme as a whole or for just one

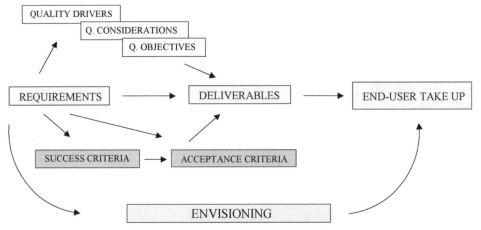

Figure 20: Requirements to end-user take-up via Envisioning

deliverable. However, whereas prototyping tends to focus on the end deliverable, envisioning goes beyond the deliverable build into its use in a user environment. Figure 20 shows the pathway from requirements to end-user acceptance. Notice the difference between this and Figure 9. It goes beyond deliverables as the end point and into the business operation.

Envisioning is a valuable aid to stakeholder expectation setting. History is littered with projects delivering technically elegant solutions that are unworkable from an end-user point of view. It is surprising to hear that even today there are projects focusing only on the delivery of the technology and not its use. 'That's not our problem' is an all too common comment from such projects.

Envisioning is not an inexpensive undertaking, since it often requires the establishment of a model environment. This could range from a complete mock-up of an office of the future or a process.

As an example of envisioning using a mock-up office, I once witnessed the establishment of a complete travel agency of the future in order to demonstrate what new technology and processes would look and feel like to those destined to operate them and also to customers.

As an example of envisioning of a process, I witnessed the set-up of an insurance claims process for a project that I managed, in order to demonstrate how novel document scanning technology could streamline a lengthy claims process. This comprised little more than one run of an office wall, with desks and equipment to show the input, throughput and output of the proposed new claims process.

These types of mock-up have implications for usability testing and also for acting as a test bed generally. In its simplest form, envisioning can be a series of drawings in a brochure or poster form, but the extent of envisioning required depends very much on the audience and culture of an organisation. Some projects feel they need to sell more than inform, so the exercise can become a grand piece of internal marketing. Many large construction projects, for example, spend considerable time and money producing detailed models of a building development. From a quality perspective it is the expectation setting that counts. At the end of the day, what is delivered needs to match the promise.

In a recent programme that I directed in the health care industry, envisioning was focused very much on the value and benefits that the end-user communities would receive from various phases of the programme. Models of benefit pathways were constructed using soft systems methodology[1]. Quantified benefits were input to a value management software tool and tracked through to take-up. The investment in a large value management and benefits group was justified by the complexity and novelty of the processes and technology being introduced by the programme. Although envisioning was through models, stakeholders were able to visualise what could be achieved and sign up for a level of benefits they felt comfortable with.

1 Refer to my book *Managing Programmes of Business Change* for details of this technique.

Prototyping

I mentioned that prototyping has a greater focus on a deliverable build. Although prototyping is a form of envisioning, since it aims to construct something resembling the features and functionality of the end deliverable, it is usually not designed to show an experience in tough practice. A prototype aircraft, for example, will not normally have all the functionality at the level required for a typical operation. It is, nonetheless, an expensive build, and many prototypes come very close to production models. A good example, in business terms, is the *pre-release* version of a piece of new software. This is often produced quickly in order to demonstrate its look and feel. However, it does not show its true potential in the working environment. In fact, even the first released version does not do this, because it will be users who will show its true potential during the weeks following release. Envisioning, however, is designed to show not just the pre-released or released software but also the ways in which it can or will be used in practice.

A typical decision that projects face when constructing something novel is whether to prototype or not. 'Will it work?' is often a fundamental question. Projects with a strong element of R&D (research and development) may feel the need to prototype in order to prove a concept. The downside of prototyping is cost and timescale. To build a prototype often lengthens the development phase of a project. Also, a prototype may significantly disappoint, bringing a re-think of the requirements and benefits. This could be a good thing in the end, but it is an expensive way to find out the truth.

Unless a prototype is fully functional it is difficult to assess performance. Some form of performance modelling is often required additionally. This can usually be accomplished with sophisticated modelling software.

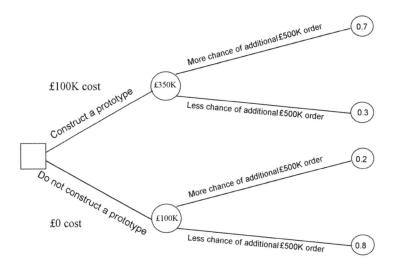

| Decision | Benefit | % Probability |

Figure 21: Decision tree to evaluate whether to construct a prototype

The benefits of prototyping are:

- early construction of a deliverable can bring confidence in the outcome to the team and stakeholders
- having a base model enables any changes to be evaluated more easily
- having a base model aids any envisioning of usage
- a prototype can act as an ongoing test bed and input to usability testing.

I recommend conducting a risk analysis to show whether prototyping is feasible for a project or not. This, in its simplest form, can show the advantages and disadvantages of prototyping, as in the decision tree shown in Figure 21. Here the benefit of building a prototype is a potential gain of £250K from an additional order from a satisfied customer. However, there is a 20%

chance of gaining the additional order without building a prototype. The additional order is actually worth £500K, but the figures shown in the chart are the expected values. Of course, other aspects need to be considered apart from just the potential gain of an additional order, such as time saved or a successful acceptance test.

Quality aspects to look for when considering prototyping are:

- Will the prototype be designed to show a working model or a mock-up for marketing purposes only?
- Will the prototype also be a test bed?
- How much effort will be required in maintaining the prototype? (ie, will changes be made, as required?)
- What is the cost/benefit for building a prototype?

Component testing

A development team will want either to test components together (integration testing) or to test them individually as they are developed. Component testing (also known as unit testing) can take different forms, depending on the nature of the components and the tolerances required. Common forms of component testing are:

- *fail-safe,* to ensure that if a component fails it does not contribute to a hazard. This is quite different from stress testing, where stress is placed on a component until it fails. The two testing types can be combined, though, if required.
- *fit for purpose*, to ensure that a component does what it is supposed to do.

Components can be hard or soft. They can be physical engineering parts, for example, or blocks of code in a software program, or even parts of a business process. Their commonality is that they form part of a whole. The whole needs to be tested as well as the individual parts.

A big problem for projects with components is control. A development team may have control over the components it develops, but when components are developed outside of a team, control is situated elsewhere. A development team would not have direct control over components developed by a third party. Even a project team relying on components being developed by its own company's manufacturing plant would not be in direct control of their development.

Where there is not direct control there is a higher risk of quality problems occurring. A project team needs to understand what testing has been done by a third party and to what degree. Some project teams prefer to re-test themselves (if they are able) third party developed components. The only real assurance of quality when dealing with third parties, however, is to maintain a close working relationship with them. Mutual trust can be gained through openness of approach and inspection of third party testing environments and procedures. Ongoing sampling is useful when the quality of manufactured components is unproven or where there are grounds to suspect that quality of manufacture has deteriorated over time.

Project teams may be able to use standard test scripts to work through or even re-use scripts from previous projects. Some scripts will have to be constructed afresh. Much testing these days is automated and may be controlled through software programs.

Quality aspects to look for when considering components, either developed in house or by a third party, are:

- Is there good, well formatted and intelligible documentation accompanying a component? (In the case of software code, is the code well commented?)

- Is there an audit trail of version control? (ie, can one component be identified against a previous version?)
- Does a component include the name of an individual responsible for its development? (ie, in order to have traceability of who constructed what)
- Are standard test scripts applicable, or do they have to be uniquely devised?

Integration testing

Integration testing is the bringing together of components to test as a deliverable or system as a whole. In some ways it emulates component testing, but the idea is to ensure that individually tested components can operate together as a whole.

An obvious example of this is a completed motor car. The many components brought together need to function as expected in the total concept of a car. These include mechanical, electro-mechanical, hydraulic, electronic and liquid components, all of which need to be tested as an integrated whole. Car manufacturers have particular test routines for this, of course, but the end result still has to meet the expectations of the end user. As I have said before, many perfectly integrated systems have failed the ultimate test – the discerning customer. Their road test will be to very different criteria than that undertaken by the manufacturing plant.

The story is the same for many items in commercial and domestic use. The business computer, the refrigerator, the television – all are subject to customer approbation. This is where the real arguments over testing tend to begin. The end customer is often only involved in this ultimate test, which places a huge burden on a manufacturer. It is not just a question of whether a product will work, but whether it will be acceptable to the marketplace.

The consideration of warranty is important in connection with integration testing, since this final form of technical test can set the level a manufacturer will place for warranty purposes. Few manufacturers will warrant usage beyond mechanical breakdown, tending to cite only normal usage for their products. Warranty is a quality consideration and needs to be established within a wide framework of cost, revenue, sales, support and resources, etc. Indications of failures during integration, stress and volume testing will help to confirm or change a view on warranty.

Integration testing of an IT system involves ensuring that there are no errors of a particular severity outstanding and that all the code hangs together and does what it is supposed to do. It is not designed to be a user test, ie, to test a user's expectations of what various functions will do. It is solely the final technical test prior to handover for user testing. It is important not to mix the two testing types together. I have witnessed many arguments over user expectations of functionality that go beyond the technical expectations. The best practice is to maintain the integrity of the change control process and follow the standard testing protocol, where user testing follows technical integration testing.

Quality aspects to look for when considering integration testing are:

- Is the deliverable or system unique, ie, have the components ever been brought together before, in this way, in this industry?
- Are standard test scripts applicable, or do they have to be uniquely devised?
- What are the warranty implications for the deliverable or system, ie, have they been predetermined, and will stakeholders consider changing them as a result of integration testing?

The considerations for version control and documentation given for component testing also apply to integration testing.

Stress testing

Stress testing is the application of pressures upon a component or an integrated system to simulate usage or extreme usage. Various forms of stress testing may be employed, and these depend on the criticality of usage in a particular environment. In considering safety aspects, for example, components may be tested well beyond any statutory limitations for operational or electrical safety.

Typical stress tests for solid components are for fire resistance, operation in extremes of temperature and robustness. Some computer manufacturers, for example, take samples off the production line and test them for robustness by dropping them from specified heights. Car manufacturers often adopt a similar approach. Also, paintwork and finishings may be tested for durability by exposure to extreme heat or extreme cold.

More flexible components, such as the paper manufactured for the production of bank notes, may be tested for survival in everyday usage. The simulation of note handling over time can be achieved by artificial distressing to determine the optimum time from new to recall. Thus, the average life of a bank note can be determined.

In the case of soft components, such as business processes or IT code, stress testing takes on different forms. A business process can be stress tested for potential bottlenecks, for example. workflow simulation software can assist with this, where a business process can be modelled and run end to end many times over. By applying additional resources or time at various points in a process, pressures on the process may be relieved.

In a business process, constraints are also stresses. For example, the need to obtain approvals or sign-offs at particular stages can put stress on a process. Businesses generally seek to reduce cycle times through a process. When examining a process end to end there are often stress points that manifest themselves, and most of these are human interactions.

IT code may be stress tested for combinations of simultaneous transactions. Programmers can see where a program or system slows because of the stress placed upon it. Instructions or processing can be reduced to accommodate various stresses.

Quality aspects to look for when considering stress testing are:

- Are there industry standards for limitations of a particular component?
- Are the limitations of a component already documented by a manufacturer?
- Do you know the limitations you want to achieve for your user environment?
- Are standard test scripts applicable, or do they have to be uniquely devised?
- Is specialist equipment needed in order to conduct a test?

Volume testing

As for stress testing, volume testing may be applied to either a component or a complete deliverable or system. Volume testing is a form of stress testing, and, like, stress testing, can take many forms. For example, a car's engine can be left running for a long period of time in order to prove continuous operation. Bank notes can be run through an automated teller machine many thousands of times to prove a similar continuous operation. Hundreds of keystrokes can be applied to a computer keyboard to simulate continuous operation and huge volumes of data can be run through software to test performance and resilience.

Volume testing can sometimes be run in conjunction with stress testing. A decision that needs to be made is: how much testing should be accomplished and for how long? If a deliverable is to be tested for *mean time to failure* then the length of testing will be uncertain at testing outset. Again, there will be warranty implications here.

Quality aspects to look for when considering volume testing are similar to stress testing:

- Are there industry standards for limitations of a particular component?
- Are the limitations of a component already documented by a manufacturer?
- Do you know the limitations you want to achieve for your user environment?
- Are standard test scripts applicable, or do they have to be uniquely devised?

User testing

Testing specifically reserved for users usually takes place after all technical tests have been completed. In certain cases, though, users are involved in ad hoc testing as deliverables are being constructed. Either way, the purpose of a user test is to verify that a product works as a user expects it to work. This is quite different from verifying that a product works technically (as discussed under *Integration testing*, above).

If envisioning has been carried out well, then a user should have a good idea of what to expect. However, envisioning cannot usually cater for detail. For example, the question: 'If I press this button does this function occur?' might well be answered through envisioning, but the fact that the button has not only to be pressed but also held down might not be conveyed through envisioning. This latter element would normally only be handled in advance through a working prototype. However, there is the possibility of surprise for a user to discover that a button has to be held down, and so not meet expectation. Interestingly, such detail would probably not have been covered in the original user requirement, unless previous experience had brought it to the forefront. I have seen a requirement voiced as: 'I want a mobile phone but I don't want to press and hold an irritatingly tiny on/off switch'. Clearly, a requirement based on experience.

User testing should be designed for change, but only change of a certain nature. It should not be an opportunity for users to make additional requirements, but only to check the usefulness of the functionality of the original requirements (or those changed under change control). Of course, there are many who think it is just such an opportunity and will seek to impose new requirements. The quality response to such an objection is to refer to a rigorous change control process. User testing is a delicate time, often requiring significant diplomacy by a project manager and team. Again, expectation setting is the key to a battle-free user test.

Some end-user education is sometimes required in order to avoid conflict during user testing. In software development projects, I have seen heated arguments develop over whether a problem encountered by a user is an incorrect requirement or a software bug. The difference between the two is very clear to a software developer, but may not be to an end-user. What is at stake, of course, is either a change that has to be made (either immediately or in a later release) because of a bug or a change of requirement that has to be accommodated under change control. With a fixed-price contract the situation is exacerbated. Some advance user education would surely help in this case.

In a construction project, it is often difficult to engage in user testing. Once a build is complete, the tendency is to move to acceptance. There are only a certain number of features that a user can test without actually moving in and making use of the new environment. For this reason, contracts tend to allow for a period of snagging. Again, this is not for new requirements, but to ensure that the existing build is acceptable in normal use.

A consideration for user testing is who will actually participate in the test. Where hundreds of users are concerned, will it be a representative sample? The Quality Plan should indicate this under the 'Test requirements' heading.

Quality aspects to look for when considering user testing are:

- How involved have users been to date?
- What expectation setting has been carried out?
- Has envisioning been undertaken or a prototype constructed?
- How novel is the deliverable? Is it unique?
- Has the change control process been rigorously applied during deliverable development? (This will have a bearing on user expectation of the accommodation of additional requirements during user testing)
- Are standard test scripts applicable, or do they have to be uniquely devised?
- Where will user testing take place – in an artificial environment or a user environment? (The Quality Plan should specify this.)

Usability testing

Many of us have struggled to assemble flat-packed furniture, following instructions that never seem to illustrate quite what to assemble; and, to further complicate matters, the instructions are often a poor translation from another language. The problem is that hardly any flat-pack kits have been tested for usability. Someone technical has written out the instructions in a way that *they* can understand, but others cannot. Even when users complain and make suggestions for improvement, the instructions are rarely updated.

Creating instructions for a mixed ability audience is difficult. The paper cat construction described in Chapter 1 proves this. It's fine if you know how, but often not obvious if you don't. Even the most commonplace instructions can be misinterpreted. There have been many who have seen the 'Don't Walk' signs on New York streets and interpreted them as 'Run'. If you don't see the corresponding 'Walk' signs it is actually not an illogical assumption to make! 'Stop' and 'Go' are far more logical instructions for the purpose.

Most problems concerning misinterpretation can be ironed out using the concept of usability testing. Usability testing became popular during the 1980s with the development of video technology at a reasonable cost. Companies like IBM saw the benefit of being able to prove user testing in an environment as near to reality as possible, particularly as a prelude to mass roll-out of deliverables. In IBM's case it was often computer hardware and software that were tested prior to roll-out.

Usability testing is carried out in a *usability laboratory*, which is characterised by two rooms divided by a one-way mirror. One room is laid out to resemble a user environment. It might be an office or a retail shop. The only main difference is the presence of at least two video cameras. The other room is equipped with video monitoring devices and a control panel. This is where developers and trainers can observe users in the other room going through the various steps of using the system to be rolled out. Figure 22 shows a typical set-up.

Figure 22: Usability laboratory (courtesy IBM UK Ltd)

The idea is for developers to be able to correct errors and make adjustments for user assumptions in the use of a system prior to mass roll-out. This can significantly reduce calls to the help desk during live deployment, since general misunderstandings of a new process and system can be ironed out beforehand. During testing, users would have access to a help desk, as in reality.

The most frequent problems tend to occur with documentation. A user manual, for example, is easily tested using a usability laboratory. Technical authors can sometimes be too close to what they are writing and may not be able to interpret procedures in a way that a user can relate to them. Their observation of users using their documentation can be quite revealing.

The use of video technology enables a running record of tests to be made. Changes made to a system, or documentation, during one test can be placed under version control and recorded accordingly. An audit trail of tapes can be produced for later comparison.

In running a usability test it is important that the users know they are being observed. They tend to disregard the cameras quite quickly when absorbed in a test. The cost of getting it right first time more than outweighs the cost of rework during roll-out. Set-up of a usability laboratory is not cheap, but it should be viewed as a permanent investment, since it can prove its worth very quickly if a company is regularly involved in roll-out projects. Alternatively, laboratories are available for hire.

It is not just technology that can be tested in a usability laboratory. Any environment where staff have to react with customers, for example, can be tested. Testing quality of service is popular these days and training staff in the principles of good service can be underwritten by usability testing.

Quality aspects to look for when considering usability testing are:

- How near to reality can an environment be established?
- What expectation setting has already been carried out?
- Has envisioning been undertaken or a prototype already constructed?
- How novel is the deliverable? Is it unique?
- Has the change control process been rigorously applied during deliverable development? (This will have a bearing on user expectation of the accommodation of additional requirements)
- Have all the interested parties come together to produce test scenarios (eg, developers, trainers, support personnel)?
- How will user representatives be selected for usability testing (eg, role, experience, geography, roll-out schedule)?

Piloting

If a usability laboratory is not available, then a similar method for roll-out projects is to run a pilot. Interestingly, the costs for usability testing and piloting are similar. A fundamental difference, however, is that a pilot is really a first installation, whereas usability testing is still perceived as only testing. What do I mean by this? Simply, that once you go out into a live user environment it is difficult to turn back if there are problems. A pilot is very visible, and could result in adverse press if problems occur.

Nonetheless, it often makes sense to run a pilot. It just needs to be well supported. I have, regrettably, seen so many pilots badly supported and left to their own devices. A pilot has to be run for a fixed period, during which specific tests have to be made. Again, I have seen projects enter a sort of permanent pilot mode, not knowing how to call a halt to piloting and take a position. Also, a pilot has to be followed by a period of assessment and adjustment, prior to mass roll-out.

Pilots have to be well planned. Many projects attempt to squeeze them into a small gap in the schedule, often because the decision to pilot is not made until quite late in the day. Adequate time has to be allowed for the collection and analysis of data, plus a review of the whole undertaking. It is worthwhile compiling a checklist of considerations in advance. What specifically should be tested in a pilot, that could not be tested elsewhere?

Quality aspects to look for when considering piloting are:

- How will a pilot site be selected?
- What expectations need to be set for users involved in the pilot?
- How disruptive will a pilot be to normal business operation at the pilot site?
- What fallback provisions can be made from the pilot to normal business operation, should a problem occur?
- Has the change control process been rigorously applied during deliverable development? (This will have a bearing on user expectation of the accommodation of additional requirements during piloting)
- Has a set of test criteria been compiled for the pilot?
- How long should the pilot last?
- Have realistic time provisions been made in the project schedule for the pilot?
- Who will review the pilot and give the go-ahead to proceed to full roll-out?

Acceptance testing

Acceptance testing is the ultimate testing activity prior to implementation and handover. However, it may be employed at key stages during a project lifespan: phase-ends or major milestones, for example. Also, a project may wish to carry out formal acceptance testing of a deliverable from a subcontractor. Criteria for acceptance are discussed in Chapter 2 and the output of acceptance testing is usually an acknowledgement by sign-off that these criteria have been met.

If adequate envisioning has been carried out throughout the life of a project then acceptance testing need not be a great surprise to an accepting stakeholder. It is those projects where stakeholders see for the first time the true extent of a deliverable that can have difficulties with gaining acceptance. Many believe that building a prototype can significantly increase the chances of stakeholder acceptance, and a balance often has to be made between the cost of building a prototype and gaining a high possibility of acceptance against not building a prototype and running the risk of a low chance of acceptance. Non-acceptance could result in significant re-work, which is itself costly.

Many acceptances are linked financially to contracts. They are, therefore, critical to achieving project success. They have a strong bearing on customer satisfaction, for, if a stakeholder does not like what he sees, a non-acceptance can damage future relations with that stakeholder. If that stakeholder is a valued customer of a company then that company ought to be interested in ensuring that acceptance testing is properly prepared, goes well and that the risks are well understood.

Accuracy and specificity of acceptance criteria are extremely important. It is often not possible to test every single aspect of a deliverable, especially software programs. A stakeholder has to be able to exercise common sense and reasonableness when signing-off acceptance of a deliverable; all the more reason to ensure that the acceptance criteria are not ambiguous. A stakeholder also has to understand the limits of his sign-off. Acceptance must be limited to the boundaries of the deliverable contained in the acceptance criteria. It is all to easy to stray from these boundaries, which is when arguments inevitably occur.

Quality aspects to look for when considering acceptance testing are:

- What expectation setting has already been carried out?
- Has envisioning been undertaken or a prototype already constructed?
- How novel is the deliverable? Is it unique?
- Has the change control process been rigorously applied during deliverable development? (This will have a bearing on user expectation of the accommodation of additional requirements during usability testing)
- Do those stakeholders having acceptance sign-off fully understand their responsibilities for sign-off? Do they know what they are looking for?

Summary

Testing is the first proof of quality. The goal is acceptance by stakeholders. The degree of testing to be undertaking depends on confidence in the product from the project and stakeholders, against the constraints of time, cost, quality and appetite for testing.

The best testing is that which is structured and shows a pathway from components to acceptable deliverable. The foundations of testing are laid even before a project commences. Stakeholder agreement to acceptance criteria and product quality should ideally be made at contract negotiation. This guarantees a baseline against which testing can be formulated.

9

Quality at implementation

By the time a project is ready for implementation, there should be no surprises about what is to be handed over. If expectation setting and envisioning have been sufficiently well undertaken, stakeholders and the user community should be ready to receive what they have expected.

If only all projects were like this! Each year we hear in the press of projects that have failed to set expectations and, almost literally, handed over deliverables on a plate! Apart from the user disappointments and frustrations with such a practice there is certainly a longer take-up of operational benefits. It seems that many project teams do not feel any ownership of their deliverables and are happy to act as mere suppliers to their own organisations. Yet, taking ownership is a form of quality, and goes beyond mere responsibility. The concept of 'total quality management' (TQM) that was popular during the late 1980s urged *all* employees of an organisation to take on mental ownership. In practice, this meant being concerned not just about one's own work but also the implications upstream and downstream in a process. An interesting analogy is the company car. When the company car breaks down, does the employee still retain the mental ownership felt at the time of delivery, or does that ownership quickly fade and the car, mentally, becomes the company's again? So much so, with implementation. A project team must dispel any feelings of 'them and us' regarding handover to a user organisation. Quality is very much concerned with partnership, even when operating under a fixed-price contract. The projects without this run the risk of poor user acceptance, and, of course, lack of follow-on work.

Handover

The quality process does not stop with testing. Preparation for implementation is an important activity that sets the seal on everything that has gone before. The manner of handover is key to user acceptance. Like the project office that sent out blanket project processes, which I described in Chapter 3, the risks are legion. Yet, it is so simple to get right.

All projects should have an implementation plan. This should describe the approach to be taken for implementation (eg, roll-out, staged conversion, teach-the-teacher, big bang), the quality elements of which should be set out in the Quality Plan. Of course, the results of any pilot stage or 'first implementation' may have meant a modification of the approach to be taken at handover.

I like to initiate a *readiness review*, which calls the implementation team and all interested parties together to check the state of readiness of the deliverables and the receiving organisation. A template can be prepared as a *statement of readiness*. Using the guidelines and questions in the template, the risks of implementation can be made apparent for decisions to be made. Many companies will have their own templates based on previous experience and relevant to particular types of project. Such templates are valuable knowledge items (as discussed in Chapter 5). At a generic level, some considerations for readiness are:

- Are the deliverables ready?
- Have all issues been resolved?
- What risks are outstanding?
- What changes are outstanding?
- Is the receiving organisation ready?
- Who will accept the deliverables on behalf of the receiving organisation?
- Has the plan for handover been drawn up and approved?
- Do external parties need to be advised (eg, press)?
- What contractual obligations have to be fulfilled (ie, formally)?
- Have stakeholders been alerted?

There is nothing much worse in implementation terms than a poor handover to a client. An otherwise good relationship can be damaged for some time through a shoddy or ill-prepared handover. If a client is clearly not ready for handover, a project manager must counsel against it, whatever the business pressures to do otherwise. Recovery from a poor handover can be slow and protracted. I remember an IT implementation of leading-edge scanning technology to users in a customer service business, which should never have taken place. A deadline is a deadline, however, and pressure from the sponsor forced the ill-fated handover to take place. While the technology operated elegantly, the users were ill-prepared for using it to operate a new business process. Chaos ensued for a few days, until the old system and process could be brought back into operation. The sponsor was quickly moved to another position, amid a flurry of customer complaints. The ultimate, successful implementation of the new process occurred some months later, after proper envisioning and training in the new process and a significant morale-repairing exercise. The mistake was recovered, but at a cost.

Ongoing quality monitoring

When the project team disbands, the receiving organisation usually has the responsibility to monitor the quality of deliverables handed over. If there is a company quality department, that function may take on the monitoring role. In a programme, there is capability within the programme to monitor quality for a period of time. However, a project team has a duty of care to ensure that provision is made for the ongoing monitoring of quality, prior to handover.

The successful delivery of quality as a concept that is built in to deliverables forms part of the realisation of benefits. So often, benefits are diluted from the moment of product handover. This may be partly because there was not sufficient attention to tracking the delivery of benefit realising components from business case to deliverable handover or the benefits were initially overstated. A project can only deliver the capability to achieve benefits. Benefits achievement is down to the user organisation. Quality, however, *can* be delivered by a project, and is a fundamental contributor to the realisation of benefits. The continual matching of quality to the statement of benefits in the business case is an important quality function for a project.

It is important to feed back experiences post-implementation to any knowledge repository (as described in Chapter 5). The lessons learned will help to guide project teams in the future to how they can improve their deliverables and implementations for better user benefits take-up.

Summary

Implementation of deliverables is a test of the robustness of any partnership between project and receiving organisation. Handover is as much a process as testing. It has to be carefully planned. A poor handover can damage a relationship between provider and client.

Quality does not end at handover. It continues into the business operation. Adequate monitoring and ongoing control need to be set in place after the project team has been disbanded.

Glossary

acceptance criteria – Ch. 2
the basis of stakeholder
acceptance of a deliverable
or component

acceptance test – a Ch. 8
formal test designed
for stakeholder acceptance
of a component or
deliverable

assumptions planning Ch. 3
– a technique to use
assumptions as a prelude
to decision-making

business change Ch. 4
manager – a formal
programme role that
prepares an organisation
for change

change control – a Ch. 6
formal process to manage
changes within a project
or programme

communications Ch.3
manager – a formal
project role to manage
communication within a
project

communication plan – Ch.3
a project document
describing how project
communication is
undertaken

component testing – Ch. 8
the testing of
individual components

configuration Ch. 6
management – a formal
means of managing the
configuration of technical
and process components

control chart – a chart Ch. 6
showing the stability of a
process within control
limits, over time

cost of quality – the Ch. 1
cost of conforming to
quality standards and
requirements and the cost
of re-work through lack
of, or poor, quality
consideration

CTQ – cost, time Ch. 2
and quality – often
expressed as a triangle of
competing attributes

decision tree – a Ch. 2
diagramming technique
to enable comparisons of
options to be made

deliverables – the Ch. 2
products built during a
project that will be
delivered into the
receiving environment

design authority – Ch. 4
a body within a project
or programme responsible
for managing the design of
what will be constructed

design manager – a Ch. 4
role in a programme or
project that is responsible
for the design of what will
be constructed. May
operate within a design
authority

document of Ch. 6
understanding – an
agreement between parties
that is not formal

earned value – a Ch. 6
technique to show the
real amount of value
earned by project tasks

envisioning – Ch. 8
demonstrating what a
concept might look like
in its end state, without
actually building it

governance – the formal Ch. 6
control of a project or
programme through reports,
reviews and boards, etc.

House of Quality – a Ch. 6
matrix balancing product
or service characteristics
with stakeholder
requirements

inspection – a means of Ch. 7
visually checking the level
of quality in a component

integration testing – Ch. 8
the testing of components
brought together

knowledge management Ch. 5
– the formal management
of information and
intellectual property that may
be deposited and re-used

lessons learned – Ch. 1
using the experiences
from previous projects to
avoid future problems

measurement criteria Ch. 5
– the basis for measuring
quality

pilot – a test in a live Ch. 8
environment, usually
prior to mass roll-out

prototyping – the Ch. 8
building of a working
model to show how
features operate, in order
to gain early buy-in and
acceptance or prove a
concept

PSA – project services Ch. **5**, 6
automation software

quality – fitness for Ch. 1
purpose; a statement of
luxury; meets expectations

quality administrator Ch. 4
– a role principally
concerned with
administering a Quality
Plan and supporting a
quality manager

quality assurance –   Ch. **7**, 4
the process of checking
that the level of quality
achieved will meet that
planned and expected

quality assurer – a   Ch. 4, 7
formal role concerned
with checking that the
level of quality achieved
will meet that planned
and expected

quality baseline – the   Ch. 3
base level of quality
agreed for a project or
part of a project

quality consideration   Ch. 2
– something that needs to
be considered in defining
the level of quality, eg,
customer care

quality control – the   Ch. 6
measurement and local
control of the desired level
of quality in a component
or deliverable

quality definition – a   Ch. 2
process to define quality
for stakeholders

quality definition map   Ch. 2
– a systemigram using
soft systems methodology
to show the pathways
from quality drivers to
quality objectives

quality definition   Ch. 2
workshop – a structured
approach to define quality
in a group session

quality driver –   Ch. 2
something that can
influence the level of quality

quality manager –   Ch. 4
a role responsible for
quality within a business,
project or programme

quality mindset –   Ch. 1
fostering the project team
and stakeholders to possess
an attitude conducive to
thinking & practising quality

quality objectives –   Ch. 2
specific objectives for
meeting quality in a project

quality plan – a   Ch. **5**, 6
project document
specifying the desired levels
of quality for deliverables

quality review – a   Ch. 7
formal review of quality
achieved as part of a
quality assurance process

quality standard – an   Ch. 2
official level of quality at
local, national or
international level

readiness review – a   Ch. 9
final review prior to
implementation

readiness statement Ch. 9
– a formal statement of
readiness prior to
implementation

requirements – Ch. 2
stakeholder needs,
formally expressed

requirements Ch. 2
breakdown structure
– a technique of
grouping requirements
into sub-categories
based on a hierarchy

re-use – re-using Ch. 1
successful material
from previous projects

security classification Ch. 6
– a means of controlling
the level of security, usually
within a document

stakeholder – someone Ch. 2
having various forms of
interest in a project

stakeholder map – Ch. **2**, 6
a matrix of stakeholder
influences and attitudes

stress testing – the Ch. 8
placing of stresses on
components or an
integrated system to
prove resilience in usage

success criteria – Ch. 2
statements of success for
a project

testing – a way of Ch. 3, **8**
proving the level of
quality in a project

usability testing – Ch. 8
testing designed to
simulate as near to
reality an operational
environment

user testing – testing Ch. 8
by users

version control – a Ch. 6
method of managing
the different versions of a
component or document

volume test – a test of Ch. 8
quantity for a component
or deliverable

walkthrough – a Ch. 7
facilitated run through a
process for the benefit
of interested parties

Bibliography

Association for Project Management (2004), *Directing Change – A Guide to Governance of Project Management*, APM, High Wycombe, ISBN 1-903494-15-X

Barkley, Bruce T. and Saylor, James H. (2001), *Customer-Driven Project Management*, McGraw-Hill, ISBN 0-07-136982-12

Bartlett, John (2002), *Managing Programmes of Business Change,* 3rd edition, Project Manager Today Publications, London, ISBN 1-900391-08-2

Bartlett, John (1992), 'Managing Business Risks in Major IT Projects', APM Journal *Project*

Brassard, Michael, & Diane Ritter (1994), *The Memory Jogger II (A Pocket Guide of Tools for Continuous Improvement & Effective Planning)*, GOAL/QPC (www.goalqpc.com)

Checkland, P.B. (1981) *Systems Thinking, Systems Practice*, John Wiley, Chichester

Harvard Business School (1998), *Harvard Business Review on Knowledge Management*, Harvard Business School Press

International Organisation for Standardisation, *ISO 9000 Quality Management Principles* (www.iso .org/iso /en/iso 9000-14000/iso 9000/qmp.html)

King, Bob (1989), *Better Designs in Half the Time – Implementing QFD Quality Deployment Function in America*, GOAL/QPC (www.goalqpc.com)

Project Management Institute (2004), *A Guide to the Project Management Body of Knowledge,* 3rd edition, Project Management Institute, USA, ISBN: 193069945X or CD-ROM from www.pmi.org

Wake, Steve (1997), *E. V.A. Earned Value Analysis – A Real Guide to Cost and Schedule Control,* Pub. Steve Wake: swake@swprojects.source.co.uk

Watson, Charles S. (1997), *Managing Projects for Personal Success,* International Thomson Business Press, ISBN 0-412-71740-9

Wilson, Brian (2000), *Systems: Concepts, Methodologies and Applications,* John Wiley & Sons Ltd, ISBN 0 471 92716 3

Wilson, Brian (2001), *Soft Systems Methodology – Concept Model Building and its Contribution,* John Wiley & Sons Ltd

Suggestions for further study

In the UK, the Association for Project Management (website: www.apm.org) is a valuable source of information for quality management in a project and programme context. Similarly, the US-based Project Management Institute (PMI) (website: www.pmi.com) also features papers and articles on quality management and has sub-groups (known as chapters) around the world.

The independent magazine, *Project Manager Today*, features regular quality management articles (website: www.pmtoday.co.uk).

Appendix A: Construction of a paper cat

The paper cat described in the Introduction is constructed as follows. See diagram overleaf.

Tip: Do not make the creases too firm, since this will hinder unravelling of the folds during inflation in Step 9.

1. Take a sheet of A4 or similar size paper. Ensure the paper is formed as a square. To form a square, take the bottom right corner and fold diagonally to the top left corner (1a). Trim off the surplus paper at the top (1c). A square remains (1d).

2. Take the bottom right corner and fold diagonally to the top left corner (as for making the square, above). Press firmly along the crease (2a). Unwrap (2b).

3. Take the bottom left corner and fold diagonally to the top right corner. Press firmly along crease (3a). Unwrap. The square paper should now be divided into four, equal, triangular partitions (3b).

4. Turn the unwrapped paper over and place it on a surface. It should not lie flat, but naturally take the shape of the roof of a house (4a). Pick up the paper and push the sides of two opposite triangular partitions into the centre (4a, 4b, 4c), while folding down the top and bottom triangular partitions. This should compress the paper into a single triangle (4d).

5. Place the triangle with the apex at the bottom (5a). Note that the triangle comprises two 'wings', front and rear, on the left side and two wings, front and rear, on the right side. Take the corner of the top right-hand front wing and fold it down towards the apex (5b). Press down, but not too firmly. Do the same with the corner of the top left-hand front wing (5c).

6. Turn the triangle round (front to back) and repeat Step 5 using the rear wing corners (6a). A small square parcel should result (6b).

153

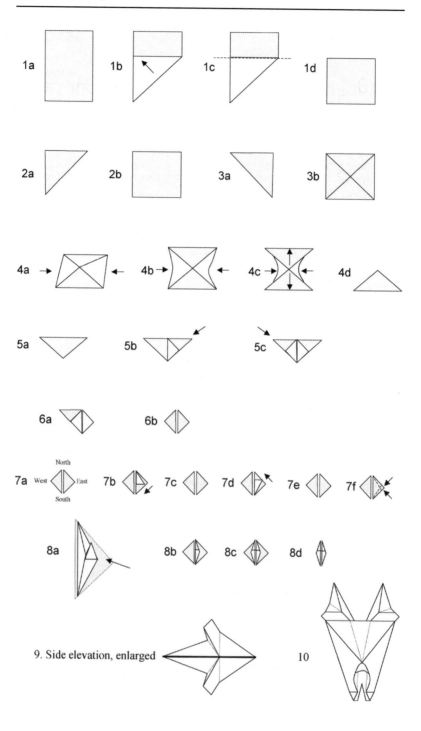

9. Side elevation, enlarged

7. Place the parcel on a surface, so that it resembles the shape in 6b. You will notice that there are four corner points. Call the points North, East, South and West (7a). Note that there are also front and rear wings, as in Step 5. Take the front wing of the East corner and fold it towards the South. (It will not reach the southern point.) Press down firmly to make a crease (7b). Unwrap what you have just done (7c). Take the front wing of the East corner again but, this time, fold it towards the North (7d). Make a crease as before. Unwrap, as before (7e). This should leave creases as shown in (7f).

8. Note the diamond-shaped crease at the extreme eastern point (7f, arrows). With your right-hand index finger and thumb grasp this crease from the right and underneath, and pinch together to make an 'ear'. Use your left-hand index finger to push against the diamond crease as you pinch, in order to ensure that the fold for the ear is made the right way round (ie, inwards towards the centre of the package and not outwards towards the East). As you pinch correctly, the folds of the wing will naturally start to push inwards. Encourage this and fold the 'ear' towards the North corner (8a: enlarged diagram of 8b). Press down to crease (8b).

   Now repeat what you have done in Steps 7 & 8 with the East front wing, but this time for the front West wing (to make 8c). Then turn over the parcel and repeat for the rear East and West sides. Pinching the paper to form the 'ears' is not easy. Try to make them even in size. Also, ensure that the 'ears' of the front side point in the same direction as the 'ears' of the rear side. A small, elongated lozenge should result, with four centrally projecting 'ears' (8d). One side forms the two ears of the cat. The other side forms the neck (ref. diagram 10).

9. Locate the end of the lozenge that has a small hole, and position the lozenge in front of you with the hole facing you. Take hold of both 'ears' from one of the sides (as in diagram 9) – grasp the left 'ear' with the left hand and the right 'ear' with the right hand. The two 'ears' remaining will represent the actual ears of the cat. Take a deep breath and blow sharply into the hole to inflate the cat shape. If inflation is difficult, assist the process by pulling up the ears. Pull down the cat's tongue.

10. The cat's head is now complete (10).

Appendix B: Completed Quality Plan example

This shows the Quality Plan format discussed in Chapter 5, completed for one deliverable.

QUALITY PLAN for *Catering Outlet Refurbishment* Project

Deliverable Name	Id	Deliverable Owner	Importance Ranking	Current Status
Cashpoint User Guide for Catering Outlets	4.14	Peter Jones, Regional Training	3	Exit Design

Owning Sub-Project	Sub-Projects Affected	Stakeholders Affected
End-User Documentation	Training; Support; Internal Marketing	Catering Outlet Managers; Regional Directors; IT Director; Support Director; Training Director; Business Change Manager

Deliverable Description

The definitive guide for catering outlets into the operation of the new electronic tills.

Components and their Origin

1. Generic operating instructions from ABC Computers Ltd.
2. Tailored operating instructions from Regional Training
3. New staff quick reference card from Regional Training
4. Help Desk and Support guidance from Regional Support

Production Cost	Maintenance Cost
1. Bundled with tills 2. 20 man days 3. 10 man days plus printing cost of £4,000 4. 25 man days 5. Combined printing: £25,000	Reprint costs for next 3 years : £8,000

Dependencies	Constraints
1. Usability testing. If UT shows up significant user difficulties with guide prior to regional rollout, then additional development time for re-work will be necessary. 2. Printing window.	1. Ref. Risk R0412007 (ABC Computers) 2. Training – high staff turnover 3. Language – high proportion of immigrant labour

Associated Requirement (s)	Stakeholder Name (s)
RQ0501006; RQ0501013	**Head of Catering** < IT Director

Deliverable Producer	Deliverable Receiver
Regional Training	Catering Outlet Managers

Integration and Usage Assumptions	Test Requirements
1. Guide will be one volume plus quick reference card 2. Hard-wearing usage in catering outlets 3. Replacement after 2 years or ad hoc	Usability Testing with representative end-users.

Acceptance & Handover Criteria	Quality Objective
User Guide can be interpreted without ambiguity by 5 users under Usability Test with production tills. User Guide will be packaged into new cash points hardware.	The User Guide will be a single A4 volume on laminated 80gsm paper, spiral bound for fold flat use, with a laminated Quick Reference Card, removable from pocket in back cover. 20 page limit, but >80% illustrative (minimum text). Two colour printing.

Measurement Criteria
Meets quality objective limits. Usability tests.

Test Sign-Off Requirements	Planned Delivery Date
Test Mgr.; Project Mgr.; Regional Catering Mgr. (for Head of Catering)	29/06/2005 for start of rollout

Quality Review Schedule

Quality Review	Date Scheduled	Date Held	Comments
End of Design	23/02/2005	23/02/2005	Report COR-QA-TR01-001
Mid-Development, prior to start of User Training specifications	25/03/2005		
End of Development, prior to Usability Testing	26/04/2005		
Post Usability Testing and prior to despatch to printing	19/05/2005		

Quality Plan Sign-Off

Name	Position	Date Agreed
Catherine W. Arnold	Head of Catering	04/01/2005

Appendix C: Draft documentation standard

Background and purpose

Documentation standards are necessary for several reasons, not least:

- to identify easily the security designation and sensitivity of a document
- to protect intellectual copyright
- to present a common format for internal and customer documentation
- to demonstrate consistency of approach
- to identify the owner and currency of a document
- to satisfy the base requirement for company quality certification.

A **document** is anything produced on behalf of our business. It could be a letter, an email, an internal procedure or form, a proposal for a customer, a brochure, a marketing flyer, or a slide presentation, for example.

It is important that everyone thinks about the appearance and sensitivity of any of the above types of document. For example, most **letters** are not confidential, and will, therefore, not require any security classification. However, since a letter projects the image of our company to a customer it should be produced in a consistent format. Templates are available to enable this consistency to be produced. Occasionally, however, a letter is confidential, and will need to be marked as such.

Similarly, **emails** are generally not confidential, and it is recommended that no confidential emails be sent over a public network without the sender being sure that they are capable of being encrypted.

Customer proposals are also documents which project the image of our company, so should follow a consistent format. They may also be customer sensitive, so may require a confidential security classification. Again, templates are available for the production of customer proposals.

Slide presentations and certain **marketing material** (such as **conference papers**) may be deemed company copyright, so should be marked © Nnn Ltd 2005 (or relevant date).

Internal forms, such as timesheets and expense forms, may not always seem confidential. However, some **become** confidential when completed. For this reason they may need to be classified as *Confidential When Completed*.

Security classification

The following three-level classification will be used for all company-produced documents:

1. *Unclassified*
2. *Confidential*
3. *Confidential Restricted*.

Documents which fall into categories 2 or 3 should bear the classification on every page. Documents which fall into category 1 (unclassified) need not contain the word *unclassified* on every page. In other words, any document which does not bear a security classification will be deemed to be unclassified by default. Most letters and emails, for example, will be in this category.

The three classification levels are explained as follows.

Unclassified

Unclassified documents are those which are not sensitive company documents, ie, if they were to fall into public hands, no damage would be done to our company. Such documents can still be company copyright, but they are not sensitive. Typical *Unclassified* documents are:

* non-sensitive letters
* public training material
* project or consultancy material for customer use
* marketing material
* some administration processes
* non-sensitive emails
* non-sensitive internal memos.

No special filing arrangements are required for *Unclassified* documents. Any of the above which contains copyright material should be marked © *Nnn Limited* followed by the year. If there is any doubt whether a document contains copyright material, err on the safe side and mark it copyright. UK copyright law is complicated and is different from North America and other regions, so could be difficult to uphold outside of the UK. However, even documents for use abroad are worthwhile protecting.

Confidential

Confidential documents are sensitive material that is designed for internal use only, and which, if landing in the wrong hands, could give a competitor useful information about the company, cause embarrassment to the company or a certain amount of business damage. Typical *Confidential* documents are:

- business plans
- profiles of customer personnel
- personnel records
- timesheets and expense claims (when completed)
- bids and proposals
- sales figures and non-public statistics
- financial analyses
- most material produced by company personnel in performing consultancy studies or projects.

Confidential material produced on behalf of a customer, such as bid responses and proposals or project plans, may be designated *Customer Confidential* instead of *Confidential* (where 'Customer' is either the name of the customer or simply left as 'Customer'). This states that the document is confidential but does not belong to our company.

Confidential documents should be filed with care. They should never be left openly visible on a desk, and always be hidden from view in a folder and stored in locked filing cabinets or briefcases. *Confidential* documents may only be sent via email if the sender is sure they are suitably encrypted.

If any *Confidential* documents contain copyright material, they should be marked: *Confidential, © Nnn Limited*, followed by the year.

Confidential Restricted

This classification is reserved for the most sensitive documents, which would definitely cause damage to our company if they fell into the wrong hands. Such documents are typically:

- company plans (eg, mergers, acquisitions, take-overs, new products, business plans)
- highly sensitive financial material.

Confidential Restricted documents must be filed securely, as for *Confidential* documents, but must also indicate the distribution list on the document (as **named individuals**). They must never be photocopied – only originals must exist. Additional copies can only be obtained from the originator. They must **never** be sent by email.

Document formatting standards

All formal documents[1] should show:

- document title on every page
- security classification on every page (but see separate provisions for *Unclassified* documents).

Customer proposals and formal documents should show, in addition:

- title page (title, author, document date, version number)
- revision and distribution data; file name (on reverse of title page)
- table of contents
- saved date, version no. and owner initials on every page.

There are no restrictions on fonts or heading styles. However, personnel producing customer proposals and bid responses should make use of the company's standard proposal templates.

Emails are not restricted in format, but should have the ability to display a security classification and/or copyright notice. Confidential emails should be sent encrypted, with the *copy protect* function enabled.

---

1 A formal document is deemed to comprise several pages and be more formal than a memorandum.

Index

Project Manager Today

P U B L I C A T I O N S

Project Manager Today Publications specialises in books and journals related to project management. Titles include:

- *Managing Programmes of Business Change*
- *Managing Risk for Projects and Programmes*
- *Managing Smaller Projects*
- *One Project Too Many*
- *The Programme & Project Support Office Handbook* vol's 1 & 2
- *Using PRINCE 2 The Project Manager's Guide*

and the flagship monthly magazine:
Project Manager Today

Publishers of *The Cost Engineer* on behalf of
The Association of Cost Engineers

Full details from:
Project Manager Today Publications
Unit 12, Moor Place Farm, Plough Lane, Bramshill, Hook
Hampshire RG27 0RF
Tel: 0118 932 6665
Fax: 0118 932 6663
www.pmtoday.co.uk

Project Manager Today also organises topical conferences and seminars.